North American
Pottery and Porcelain

Ex Líbrís

ann marie Beem

Other Titles in the Warner Collector's Guides Series

Available Now

The Warner Collector's Guide to American Toys
The Warner Collector's Guide to American Longarms
The Warner Collector's Guide to American Quilts
The Warner Collector's Guide to American Clocks
The Warner Collector's Guide to North American Pottery and
Porcelain
The Warner Collector's Guide to American Sterling Silver and
Silver-Plated Hollowware
The Warner Collector's Guide to Pressed Glass
The Warner Collector's Guide to Dolls

The Warner Collector's Guide to
North American
Pottery and Porcelain

Ellen and Bert Denker

A Main Street Press Book

WARNER BOOKS

A Warner Communications Company

R
29

Warner Books, Inc.
75 Rockefeller Plaza
New York, NY 10019

 A Warner Communications Company

Printed in the United States of America

First printing, June 1982

10 9 8 7 6 5 4 3 2 1

Library of Congress Cataloging in Publication Data

Denker, Ellen.
  The Warner collector's guide to North American pottery and
porcelain.
  (The Warner collector's guides)
  Bibliography: p. 250
  Includes index.
  1. Pottery—North America—Collectors and
collecting.   2. Porcelain—North America—
Collectors and collecting.   I. Denker, Bert,
joint author.   II. Title.
NK4003.D46   738'.097   80-25230
ISBN 0-446-97631-8 (USA)
ISBN 0-446-37092-4 (Canada)

Contents

How to Use This Book

The purpose of this book is to provide the collector with a visual identification guide to North American pottery and porcelain. Although numerous books have been written concerning individual aspects of the potter's art—throwing techniques, glazes, decoration, important makers and designers—the fifty guide categories in this unique guide provide even the most inexperienced collector with a synthesis of all the important features necessary to identify and classify pottery and porcelain.

The broadest possible way to classify pottery and porcelain is by **type of ceramic body**—that is, what type of clay was used? This classification roughly parallels the history and development of the ceramic industry, from the early production of coarse wares, to the more refined manufacture of porcelain. These broad categories have been subdivided, in turn, according to the **style and type of decoration** applied to the ceramic body (sgraffito, slip-trailed, brush-painted, etc.). An exception must be applied to art potteries, which are made of such a variety of bodies (known only by chemical analysis), that they have been divided by **factory or region** as a useful guide to regional collectors. In fact, location assumes an important role in classifying several of the other categories also, since regional variations were common even within a particular decorative technique (New England slip decoration, Pennsylvania slip decoration, etc.).

Use of this collector's guide is designed with ease, speed, and portability in mind. Suppose you spot a ceramic vase that appeals to you at a flea market or in an antique shop. The piece feels light and appears to be made of porcelain. Perhaps the dealer has told you the obvious: "It is a Victorian porcelain vase." But there must have been hundreds of porcelain pieces produced throughout North America in the late 19th century. What kind of porcelain body is it? What potter or pottery is responsible for its manufacture? When was it made? Is its decoration common to other porcelain pieces? Was it made for a specific purpose or person? These are just a few of the many questions that you may want answers to.

By turning to the Color Key to North American Pottery and Porcelain (pp. 16-48), you will find among the fifty color illustrations a photograph of a porcelain piece that bears a close "family resemblance" to the one you're interested in—the visible characteristics, the basic shape, are definitely similar. Under the color illustration will be found the number and name of the classification. By turning to the number and chapter heading in the body of the book which corresponds with the color photograph (32. Porcelain: Victorian), you will be able to find either the identical piece or pieces very similar to it. By turning to the pages in the body of the book, you will discover, among other things, the piece's probable maker, its date and place of manufacture, a concise and detailed description of its shape, decoration, and distinctive markings, and its approximate value.

Using this guide, then, is very simple. To repeat: once you find a piece of pottery or porcelain that you want to find out more about, simply turn to the Color Key (pp. 16-48), find the color photograph that most closely identifies the classification of your ceramic piece, and turn to the pages indicated for further information.

Each of the 500 pieces of pottery and porcelain discussed in this guide is treated in a separate numbered entry, containing basic information. A typical entry is reproduced on p. 9, together with a list of all the basic elements contained in each entry of the book. Most of these elements are self-explanatory, but the reader should take note of several areas.

Marked Pieces: As many signed pieces as possible have been included in this guide because these furnish the most secure documents for attribution of unsigned pieces; however, it should be remembered that American pottery is not always signed, particularly the early coarse wares made for local consumption.

Price Range: This is a treacherous area, so let no one fool you into thinking that any so-called price guide is a completely accurate means of determining the value of a piece of pottery. Essentially, a piece is worth whatever a collector is willing to pay for it. Still, there have to be guidelines, and this guide offers not prices, per se, but **price ranges** based on the following considerations: (1) that the piece of pottery or porcelain is in perfect or near perfect condition, particularly for pieces made within the last 100 years; (2) pottery prices are often dependent on the region of origin. Collector interest and the valuation of Indiana stoneware, for example, will necessarily center in that state; (3) marked examples are more desirable, and therefore more valuable than unmarked examples, which means that unmarked examples comparable to illustrations here would have a lower value than the range indicated by the letter code; (4) many museum objects have been used as illustrations because they were readily available and provide good documents; the value ranges assigned, however, should not be constructed as prices for the particular objects illustrated, but are only suggestive of the **type** of ceramic piece in the entry. The price ranges suggested in this guide are coded as follows:

A — under $100
B — $100 to $250
C — $250 to $500
D — $500 to $1000
E — over $1000

Note: The National Museum of American History, Smithsonian Institution, Washington D.C., is abbreviated "NMAH" and appears often as the source line throughout the text.

A Typical Entry

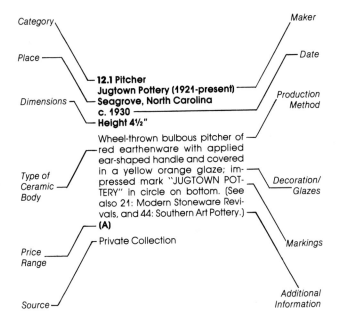

Category

Place

Dimensions

Type of
Ceramic
Body

Price
Range

Source

Maker

Date

Production
Method

Decoration/
Glazes

Markings

Additional
Information

**12.1 Pitcher
Jugtown Pottery (1921–present)
Seagrove, North Carolina
c. 1930
Height 4½"**

Wheel-thrown bulbous pitcher of
red earthenware with applied
ear-shaped handle and covered
in a yellow orange glaze; impressed mark "JUGTOWN POT-
TERY" in circle on bottom. (See
also 21: Modern Stoneware Revivals, and 44: Southern Art Pottery.)
(A)
Private Collection

Introduction

In our daily lives we are surrounded by objects made of clay. From the ceramic tile and sanitary fixtures of the bath to the plates on the table, we are constantly in contact with the potter's craft, although often in highly mechanical forms. In the past, too, ceramics of all kinds were in regular use. They included the finest porcelain teacups, as well as the cheapest redware chamber pot. Although Americans during the last 300 years have continued to enjoy ceramic wares of foreign manufacture, much of what we have consumed has been made on this continent. The task, then, of compiling a guide to North American pottery is enormous.

For the ceramics enthusiast there are many books available on specialized subjects. Collectors interested in the rare, early porcelains produced by Bonnin and Morris of Philadelphia, as well as admirers of the common florists' crockery made at the Hull Pottery in Ohio, will find articles and books to escort them through the intricacies of identification and appreciation of many specific types of pottery.

On the other hand, this volume is general in nature. The goal has not been to list every ceramic object made in America, but to recommend useful methods for recognizing wares that will lead the reader on the path to further study. Certain types of ceramics are not discussed for several reasons. Indian pottery and the wide variety of limited editions made in this century will be explored in separate future volumes. In addition, some of the earliest American-made wares are mentioned only briefly because they are known primarily from archaeological evidence and thus are too rare to be found on the market today. Porcelain plumbing and electrical fixtures are also beyond the scope of this volume.

The first step in identifying a particular example of pottery is to determine the composition of the body. The major divisions of this guide, therefore, are based on the types of ceramic bodies, while subdivisions are defined by the processes and styles of decoration borne by the body.

Pottery can be divided into three primary categories based on the character of the body, or ceramic fabric, of the object. Red, yellow, and white earthenwares are coarse, soft, easily scratched and broken, opaque, and generally rather thickly made. Stonewares are also coarse, opaque, and heavily made, however, they are much more durable than earthenwares because stoneware clays may be fired to vitrification or impermeability. Porcelains are finely grained and also quite sturdy. They are often distinguished from stonewares by their translucency. The visual distinctions in these wares reflect the variety of clays utilized, as well as differences in the manufacturing processes. Earthenwares, for example, require much less heat in firing and often less stringent concern for cleanliness during preparation of the clay than do porcelains.

In order to understand the importance of any particular type of pottery, a whole picture of the development of the North American ceramic industry must be taken into account. This development, in fact, roughly follows the hierarchy inherent in these three types of ceramic body.

During the seventeenth and eighteenth centuries, American potters were most concerned with production of the cheap, coarse
wares. Hundreds of potteries turned out the many utilitarian objects
needed for household and dairy activities. For the most part, these
wares were made in a limited number of shapes—jugs, mugs, bowls,
jars, plates, and pots. Because these were traditional forms which
had been reduced over a long period of time to their most useful
shapes, potters everywhere produced very similar wares. Obviously,
details of manufacture differed from potter to potter, but, in most
cases these differences are so subtle that they can rarely be used to
make firm attributions of undecorated pottery to a particular known
potter. Decorated earthenwares and stonewares, however, exhibit
variations which have been identified for particular regions. These
distinguishing characteristics are discussed under the separate
categories.

The availability of clays, consumer markets, and transportation all
played major roles in the development of the ceramic industry in a
particular region. A competent potter, for example, who discovered
suitable clays on his property and was located near a well-traveled
land or water route, could provide nearby customers with a desirable
and inexpensive product. The widespread availability of clays ap-
propriate for producing red earthenwares combined with the general need for cheap household and dairy forms meant that redware
potteries were viable in almost any area. Less common stoneware
clays, however, required more sophisticated and costly processing
into marketable forms. Early stoneware potteries, therefore, tended to
be located near major sources of clay (northeastern New Jersey,
Manhattan, Staten Island, and northern Ohio) or near major waterways along which heavy clays could be inexpensively transported
(the Hudson River and Erie Canal in the Northeast).

The need for more sophisticated technology also played a major
role in the centralization of potteries specializing in the production of
brown- or rockingham-glazed yellow earthenwares. The successful
manufacture of these wares, which began in the early nineteenth
century, was made possible by the use of plaster molds manipulated
through a complex division of labor within the pottery.

The production of fine table and ornamental porcelain is considered the highest plateau attainable in the ceramic industry. The
Chinese product, much admired by Westerners, was not successfully
duplicated in Europe until the early eighteenth century. The need for
specialized clays and manufacturing processes, combined with a
rather elite consumer market (which preferred the foreign products),
contributed to the painfully slow emergence of the porcelain industry
in North America.

The manufacture of porcelain in America during the late eighteenth and early nineteenth centuries was of a highly experimental
nature. The Philadelphia firm of Bonnin and Morris, for example, survived only two years. For some companies from this period no known
examples are extant. By 1875, however, the industry began to cluster
around Trenton, New Jersey, and East Liverpool, Ohio. In addition, the
rapid influx of many skilled potters from the English and German
ceramic industries put the American enterprises on a footing which
was more competitive with foreign products.

Parallel with the slow development of fine porcelain manufacture in America during the nineteenth century was a flourishing white ware industry. The term white ware refers to a variety of white, or nearly white, ceramic bodies ranging from refined earthenwares to semi-porcelain. Wares included in this category were given many similar names: opaque porcelain, stone china, white granite, Paris granite, ironstone, and semi-vitreous porcelain. While the composition of each type differs slightly from another, all of the wares are opaque because either the coarseness of the clay or the thickness of the potting does not permit translucency. In this branch of the ceramic industry, as well, the major centers of production were Trenton and East Liverpool. Common table and toilet wares, mass-produced in slip and jigger molds, constituted the production lines of white ware potteries.

During the late nineteenth and early twentieth centuries an aesthetic movement challenged the conventional approach to interior decoration. In ceramics this movement showed itself in a concern for ornamental forms (vases, jardinieres, plaques, etc.) which were made and decorated entirely by hand or which, at least by their style, gave the impression of having been made by hand. These wares, recognized more by their appearance than by their composition, are most commonly made of various stoneware bodies, highly refined earthenwares, or, more rarely, porcelain. In form they are often organic, based on the structural manipulation of vegetal models, or have elegant, classical shapes. Glazes range from deep glossy browns and rich matte earthtones to brilliant red and blue flambé effects. Widespread experimentation yielded an enormous variety of glazes and forms. The company able to develop and market a particular "look" to a large audience was very successful. Alongside the relatively large and long-lived operations—such as the Weller Pottery, the Newcomb College Pottery, or the Van Briggle Pottery—were those smaller companies or single potters whose products achieved only limited popularity. For example, George E. Ohr of Biloxi, Mississippi, hailed today as one of the greatest American potters, sold little of his most brilliant work.

During this same period the popular desire for aesthetic decoration resulted in an enormous tile industry in England and Europe, as well as in America. While the tradition of using decorative tiles for interior and exterior floors and walls goes back at least as far as the fourth millenium B.C. in the ancient Near East, their use in Europe did not occur to any degree until late in the twelfth century A.D. In America, the widespread popularity of tiles for every space from foyers to bathrooms did not emerge until the late nineteenth century. In fact, the market for tiles had become so large by 1900 that many companies produced nothing else.

Out of the factory-like studio setting of such well-known establishments as the Rookwood Pottery in Cincinnati, Ohio, emerged the single artist-potter, or studio potter, after the turn of the century. Primarily supported by universities and art schools since the 1930s, these potters have been free to explore the ceramic medium with few of the financial constraints which might plague a commercial operation. For the ceramic artist, therefore, the product reflects personal exploration and expression rather than popular taste.

MARKS

Although marks on pottery can be misleading, they are also extremely useful when they are impressed, incised, or printed on an
authentic piece. Having first established the general period of manufacture through examination of the object and visual or mental comparison with other similar objects, the connoisseur then looks to the
mark for confirmation. Edwin AtLee Barber's 1904 volume **Marks of
American Potters** is still the most valuable guide to marks on American pottery made before 1900. Since Barber's work, little effort has
been directed toward systematically researching and recording
twentieth-century marks, making positive identification of the manufacturer a difficult task in this later period.

Because redwares were made primarily for local markets, it is rare
to find an example with a mark. The markets for stoneware, however,
were much more competitive and generally encompassed a wider
area than redware. It is more common to find pieces of stoneware
with manufacturers' marks which were used as a type of advertising,
as well as a method of giving the consumer the impression that the
stoneware was of a higher quality (in the same way that brand names
are supposed to accomplish the same goals today).

Manufacturers' marks are sometimes intended to mislead the consumer. During the third quarter of the nineteenth century, for example, many white ware companies in Trenton and East Liverpool used
pseudo-English marks to give the customer the impression that they
were buying the more highly esteemed foreign product. Often these
marks resemble the coat of arms of Great Britain with rampant lion
and unicorn holding a shield between them, although some manufacturers, such as the East Trenton Pottery Company, used the arms of
New Jersey to achieve the same effect.

The connoisseurship of American and Canadian ceramic products
is a complex process. No novice can expect to become an expert
overnight. By looking at examples critically, asking questions of
knowledgeable dealers, collectors, and museum curators, and
studying the wealth of published and unpublished documentary
material, an enthusiast can gain much insight into the subject.

Color Key to North American Pottery and Porcelain

1. Redware: Plain Utilitarian

2. Redware: Sgraffito Decoration

3. Redware: New England Slip Decoration

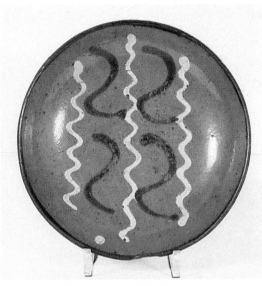

4. Redware: Pennsylvania Slip Decoration

5. Redware: New Jersey Slip Decoration

6. Redware:
Shenandoah
Valley Slip
Decoration

7. Redware:
New York
Slip
Decoration

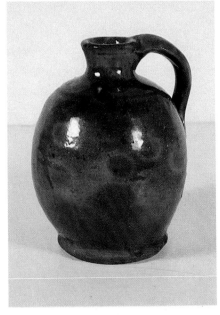

Above:
8. Redware:
Moravian
Slip
Decoration

9. Redware:
Colored
Glazes

10. Redware: Molded and Modeled

Below:
11. Redware: Canadian

12. Redware: Modern Revivals

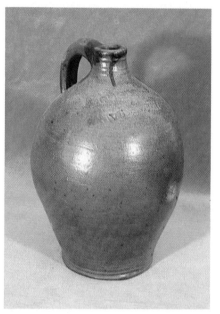

13. Stoneware:
Plain
Utilitarian

14. Stoneware:
Incised or
Impressed
Decoration

Above:
15. Stoneware:
Slip-trailed
Decoration

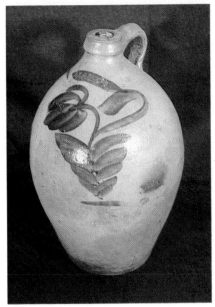

16. Stoneware:
Brush-painted
Decoration

17. Stoneware:
Stenciled
Decoration

18. Stoneware:
Alkaline
Glazes

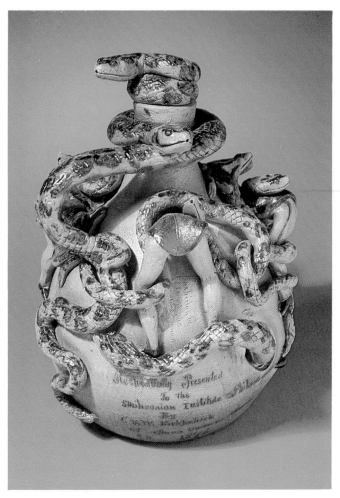

19. Stoneware: Molded and Modeled

Above:
20. Stoneware:
Canadian

21. Stoneware: Modern
Revivals

22. Yellow Ware: Rockingham

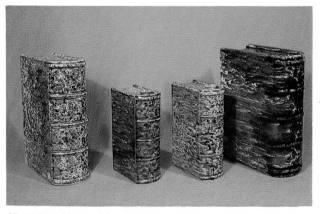

23. Yellow Ware: Bennington

24. Yellow Ware: Plain and Colored Glazes

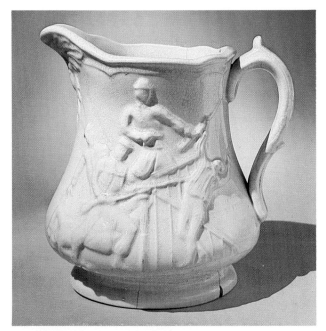

25. White Ware: Plain Molded

26. White Ware: Printed Tablewares

27. White Ware: Printed Toilet Wares

28. White Ware: Printed Commercial ana
Commemorative

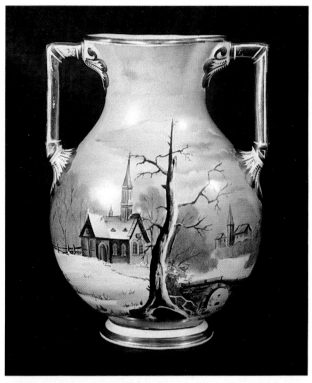

29. White Ware: Hand Painted

30. Porcelain: Eighteenth Century

31. Porcelain: Empire

32. Porcelain: Victorian

33. Porcelain: Parian

34. Porcelain: Late Victorian

35. Porcelain: Victorian, Trenton

36. Porcelain: Modern

37. Art Pottery: Rookwood

Above:
38. Art
Pottery:
Weller

39. Art
Pottery:
Rozane/
Roseville

40. Art Pottery:
Other Ohio
Potteries

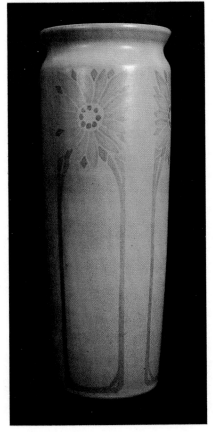

41. Art Pottery:
New England

42. Art Pottery: New York State

43. Art Pottery: Mid-Atlantic

44. Art Pottery: South

Above:
45. Art Pottery:
California

46. Art Pottery:
Colorado

47. Art
Pottery:
Great
Lakes

48. Modern
Studio
Pottery

49. Tiles

50. Modern Tableware

1 | Redware: Plain Utilitarian

Redware pottery is made from the gray or blue gray alluvial clay commonly found in a great many parts of the country. Once the sticks, stones, and other impurities were cleaned out, this raw material could be formed on a simple potter's wheel into the numerous utilitarian wares needed for cooking, storage, dairying, and construction. Vessels were usually glazed with a mixture of red lead, silica sand, and water in order to render the porous redware impermeable to liquids. In the case of bricks, drainage pipes, and tiles, the material was left unglazed.

As a result of recent archaeological excavations in Virginia at Carter's Grove near Colonial Williamsburg, it is evident that redware was manufactured at least as early as the 1630s in the American colonies. Few industries in the colonies were encouraged by England as the motherland sought to protect the markets for English potters (and other manufacturers), but local need, frugality, and capitalist instincts provided incentive for craftsmen to establish small potteries in many villages.

The basic pottery forms were those found in England, Germany, and other regions where potters had learned their craft. Certain shapes can be traced back to their origins hundreds of years earlier. Sometimes the pieces were decorated with slip designs, colored glazes, or fancy molded patterns, but most of these wares were simply lead-glazed. Modest decoration consisted of incised or coggled bands, although the pieces were designed primarily to perform a function and enable the potter to sell them at an affordable price. Consumers did not demand more than the beauty of an honestly crafted object for their basic utilitarian redware.

1.0 Jar (color plate)
Probably Pennsylvania, 1850-1870
Height 9⅝"

Wheel-thrown, slightly ovoid jar of red earthenware with manganese/lead glaze burned almost black and left to drip around the lower half. Excellent example of this very common black-glazed redware typical of the Middle Atlantic region. **(A)**

Private Collection

1.1 Preserve Jar
Henry H. Ziegler (working 1852-1865)
Newville, Pennsylvania, 1852-1865
Height 5½", Diameter 5⅛"

Wheel-thrown ovoid jar of red earthenware, prominent lip; lead glaze with green-gray tint overall; impressed mark on bottom "H.H. ZIGLER [sic] /NEWVILLE PA." **(A)**

1.2 Jar
Cyrus Cornell
East Aurora, Erie County,
  New York, c. 1835
Height 12½"

Wheel-thrown ovoid jar of red earthenware glazed on interior and exterior; mark impressed below rim "C. CORNELL/AURORA." **(B)**

Collection of Kathleen S. and George R. Hamell

1.3 Jar
Eastern United States
1825-1875
Height 9"

Wheel-thrown cylindrical jar of red earthenware with small applied handles, raised coggled band below rim, and black-tinted lead glaze. **(A)**

NMAH

1.4 Crock
Emanuel Suter (working c. 1855-1890)
Harrisonburg, Virginia, c. 1855-1870
Height 8⅜"

Wheel-thrown, slightly ovoid crock of red earthenware with modeled band at rim; glazed interior with brown Albany slip; impressed mark near rim "E. SUTER." **(A)**

1.5 Jug
Probably Haddonfield,
  New Jersey, c. 1780
Height 7"

Wheel-thrown ovoid jug of red earthenware; strap handle; streaky brown-tinted lead glaze overall. **(B)**

National Gallery of Art, Index of American Design

1.6 Jug
Daniel Bayley
Newburyport, Massachusetts
1764-1799
Height 9"

Wheel-thrown ovoid jug of red earthenware; applied strap handle; streaky brown and clear lead glaze overall. **(B)**

NMAH

1.7 Jug
Alexander Boughner
   (active c. 1812-1850)
Greensboro, Pennsylvania, 1849
Height 8¹/₁₆"

Wheel-thrown, squat ovoid jug of red earthenware with applied strap handle; brown-tinted lead glaze overall. **(A)**

NMAH

1.8 Batter Jug
Samuel Daily (working 1868)
York County, Pennsylvania, 1868
Height 10¾"

Wheel-thrown and modeled globular jug of red earthenware with two tubular spouts at top on each side of a strap handle; streaky brown-tinted lead glaze; impressed mark "S.L. DAILY". **(B)**

1.9 Plate
Lewis K. Tomlinson (working c. 1850-1889)
Dryville, Berks County, Pennsylvania, c. 1875
Height 1½"; Diameter 7¾"

Drape-molded round plate of red earthenware with clear lead glaze on front only; impressed "LKT" in an oval on the bottom. **(A)**

1.10 Food Mold
Eastern Pennsylvania, 1840-1900
Height 3⅛"; Diameter 7¼"

Molded baking mold of red earthenware with fluted sides and scalloped top rim, covered in a brown-
spotted, clear lead glaze. **(A)**

National Gallery of Art, Index of
American Design

1.11 Cake Mold
James and Thomas Haig (1831-1878)
Philadelphia, Pennsylvania, c. 1850
Diameter 9"

Red earthenware "turk's head" mold; fluted design with brown spots
and clear lead glaze overall; impressed mark "J. & T. HAIG" on rim. **(B)**

1.12 Wash Basin
Salem, North Carolina, 1775-1850
Height 7"; Diameter 19¼"

Round, wheel-thrown wash basin
with straight, flaring sides, characteristic double-ridge rim, applied
handles; brown lead-glazed interior only. **(B)**

Old Salem Restoration

1.13 Wash Bowl and Pitcher
Probably Solomon Purdy (working c. 1834-1850)
Zoar, Tuscarawas County, Ohio, Dated 1840
Height, pitcher 11⅛"; Diameter, bowl 17"

Wheel-thrown redware bowl and pitcher, large handles on bowl, clear
lead glaze on interiors only; "ZOAR" impressed on handle of bowl with
stars and "1840". **(D, set)**

1.14 Pitcher
Harford County, Maryland
Early 19th century
Height approximately 12"

Wheel-thrown red earthenware
pitcher with bulbous body and incised lines at shoulder, slightly flaring vertical neck, grooved strap
handle, silvery lead glaze streaked
with black. **(B)**

NMAH

1.15 Bowl
Eardley Brothers Pottery
St. George, Utah, c. 1855
Size unknown

Wheel-thrown redware bowl with a flat rim, covered in dark lead glaze. Possibly a wash bowl. **(B)**

National Gallery of Art, Index of American Design

1.16 Teapot
Thomas Crafts
  (working c. 1802-1820)
Whately, Massachusetts, c. 1820
Height 6"

Wheel-thrown teapot with applied molded spout, extruded and applied handle; covered in a lustrous black manganese and lead glaze. **(B)**

NMAH

1.17 Mug
Attributed to Essex County,
  Massachusetts, 1800-1825
Height 5⅞"

Wheel-thrown mug with incised line at top and bottom, applied ear-shaped handle, brown-tinted lead glaze overall. **(B)**

NMAH

1.18 Grease Lamp
Justus Blaney
Cookstown, Pennsylvania
1825-1854
Height 5⅝"

Wheel-thrown redware lamp with saucer base, single spout, applied strap handle; covered in black lead glaze; impressed mark on bottom "Justus Blaney/Cookstown, Pennsylvania." **(C)**

National Gallery of Art, Index of American Design

2 | Redware: Sgraffito Decoration

Redware decorated by the "sgraffito" method is highly valued by collectors. The term is derived from the Italian for "to scratch" and describes the technique of incising (scratching) a design through a thin layer of light-colored slip applied over the slightly damp, unfired pot. All of the pottery with sgraffito decoration was specially produced in limited quantities and, therefore, more expensive than the undecorated utilitarian wares.

The German potters who came to the eastern Pennsylvania counties of Bucks, Montgomery, and Chester in the late eighteenth and early nineteenth centuries were proud practitioners of this decorative technique. Some of the designs, in fact, are almost indistinguishable from the ones used in Germany at the same time. Sgraffito-decorated ware was also very popular in the Devonshire area of England and some of that influence can be seen in American examples by Joseph Smith of Pennsylvania and a unique plate by Phillip Durell of New Jersey.

In 1903 the pioneer scholar and collector, Edwin AtLee Barber, wrote **Tulip Ware of the Pennsylvania-German Potters.** As a result, the relatively few remaining examples of this fragile pottery were avidly pursued, and today, the supply available to collectors is quite small. Authentic eighteenth- and nineteenth-century pieces made in Germany have been brought to America in the last twenty years. Though scarce also, the German products pose the most serious threat to the unwary buyer. The most commonly found examples of this technique are those made by the American-Revival potters of the twentieth century (see category 12 Redware: Modern Revivals).

2.0 Plate (color plate)
Johannes Neesz
Tylersport, Montgomery County, Pennsylvania, 1810-1820
Diameter approximately 12"

Drape-molded red earthenware plate decorated with sgraffito design of horse and rider surrounded by tulips and fuchsia with German inscription that translates "I have been riding over hill and dale and everywhere have found (pretty) girls." **(E)**

NMAH

2.1 Plate
"R.G."
Eastern Pennsylvania
Dated 1815
Diameter 11½"

Drape-molded plate with sgraffito decoration depicting elaborate vase of flowers with diamond ground; flowers have cross-hatched centers. **(E)**

NMAH

2.2 Plate
Phillip Durell (working c. 1780-1800)
Elizabeth, Union County, New Jersey
Dated "October 27th, 1793"
Diameter 13½"

Drape-molded red earthenware plate, front covered in white slip with sgraffito decoration of three flowers with leaves, inscribed "Manufactured by/Phillip Durell" and date. **(E)**

2.3 Plate
Possibly John Monday
Eastern Pennsylvania, c. 1825
Diameter 11¾"

Sgraffito-decorated red earthenware plate with incised parrot and flowers with green spots. **(E)**

2.4 Plate
Conrad Ranninger (c. 1835-1845)
Montgomery County, Pennsylvania, Dated 1838
Diameter 9⅝"

Red earthenware plate with unusual negative stencils of a large horse, small heart, and double eagle; scratched into front and back "Conrad K. Ranninger, June the 23, 1838." **(E)**

2.5 Dish
Samuel Troxel (active 1823-1833)
Montgomery County, Pennsylvania, Dated 1823
Length 9⅓"

Drape-molded oval dish of red earthenware with fluted sides; sgraffito design of pot with flowers, Pennsylvania-German inscription and date around border; unmarked. **(E)**

2.6 Covered Jar
Jacob Scholl
Tylersport, Montgomery County,
   Pennsylvania, c. 1830
Height 9"

Wheel-thrown cylindrical jar having white slip ground with sgraffito floral design and cobalt blue and copper green highlights. **(E)**

National Gallery of Art, Index of American Design

2.7 Bowl
Thomas Vickers (1757-1829)
Chester County, Pennsylvania, Dated 1802
Height 4"; Diameter 9 1/8 "

Wheel-thrown footed bowl of red earthenware with transparent green glaze overall; decorated with sgraffito design of random flowers and "1802" and "Molly Dorat" in wreaths on outside; incised script mark "Vickers" on bottom. **(E)**

2.8 Flowerpot and Saucer
Enos Smedley (working 1829-1854)
Chester County, Pennsylvania, Dated April 3, 1826
Height 10 1/4 "

Wheel-thrown and modeled flowerpot and saucer of red earthenware with scalloped and crimped edges, applied white slip on saucer; presentation inscription on side of pot; signed "Enos Smedley, Westtown" on bottom of saucer. **(E)**

3 | Redware: New England Slip Decoration

A distinctive method of decorating redware was to "trail" white slip, a liquid clay, on a partially dry piece of pottery and, then, after a short wait, to press the somewhat hardened slip decoration into the ware. A much less common method of using slip to ornament redware was simply to paint it directly onto the surface of a piece.

The technique of slip trailing, accomplished with a small pottery cup fitted with one or more quills, was utilized before 1700 in Massachusetts. The English influence on decoration was dominant throughout New England, while the German sgraffito methods were prevalent in eastern Pennsylvania. Most of the examples of slip-trailed redware found in New England were made in southwestern Connecticut and the Connecticut River Valley, where the popularity of these wares survived until the middle of the nineteenth century. The most significant differences in style among the various New England slip-decorated wares are the result of the influence of potters from Pennsylvania and New Jersey who carried their designs to southwestern Connecticut. Other New England potteries featured brushed or combed slip decoration in the English tradition.

Pie plates and shallow oval dishes are still readily available to the collector. The complexity of design or rarity of inscription help to determine the price. The simple "ABC," "Lemon Pie," or "Mary's Dish" notation on a piece is much more common than, for example, "Washington," a flower, or a rare "1764" date. The abstract linear designs, while quite attractive and occasionally inspired, appeal to fewer collectors and, consequently, may be found at a lower price.

3.0 Dish (color plate)
Attributed to Joseph Wilson
Dedham, Massachusetts, Dated 1764
Diameter 11⅜"

Wheel-thrown red earthenware dish with bands of dark brown and light slip decoration. **(E)**

NMAH

3.1 Pan
Probably Exeter, New Hampshire
Dated 1830
Diameter 13½"

Red earthenware pan, slip-decorated with concentric lines of white and dark brown slip with lead glaze; legend in center "DmA/ 1830"; made as a christening present for Dorothy Melissa Ann Goodrich of East Kingston, New Hampshire. **(D)**

NMAH

3.2 Plate
Norwalk, Connecticut, c. 1825
Diameter 10"

Drape-molded red earthenware plate with linear slip-trailed design. **(C)**

NMAH

3.3 Plate
Probably Connecticut, c. 1840
Diameter 9⅛"

Drape-molded red earthenware plate with slip-trailed legend "Lemon/Pie", clear lead glaze overall. **(D)**

Private Collection

3.4 Jug
Unidentified Maker
New England, 1790-1825
Height 5¼"

Small, wheel-thrown ovoid jug of
red earthenware with large white
slip spots and random green
splashes; clear lead glaze overall. **(D)**

Nancy & Gary Stass Collection

3.5 Chamber Pot
Daniel Bayley Pottery
Newburyport, Massachusetts
1764-1799
Height 6"

Wheel-thrown red earthenware
chamber pot with white slip
brushed on in whorls; light green
lead glaze. **(C-D)**

NMAH

4 | Redware: Pennsylvania Slip Decoration

Slip-decorated redware in the Pennsylvania tradition is often confused with the similar New Jersey and New England types. The deeper
profile of the dish, more pronounced coggling of the edge, and
thicker slip lines of the Pennsylvania pie plates and pans, however,
distinguish them from those made in other areas. Certain slip-trailed
designs such as the tulip, "distelfink," and Germanic inscriptions are
only found on Pennsylvania redware and on some pottery made by
the Moravians in North Carolina.

The popularity of this method of decorating survived well into the
nineteenth century in Connecticut, and was also practiced quite late
by some Pennsylvania potters. Some of these later redware plates
made in Pennsylvania were thrown on a potter's wheel rather than
formed by draping a flat, circular "pancake" of damp clay over a
mold. The New England potters, on the other hand, seem to have used
the "drape-mold" technique almost exclusively after 1800. The

thrown plates are never completely smooth, but show slight ridges on the outside created by the hands of the craftsman.

4.0 Plate (color plate)
Willoughby Smith
Womelsdorf, Pennsylvania, c. 1850-80
Diameter 8½"

Shallow drape-molded plate decorated with slip-trailed linear design in yellow and brown with clear lead glaze overall. Impressed mark "W. SMITH / WOMELSDORF" on bottom. **(C)**

Nancy & Gary Stass Collection

4.1 Plate
Eastern Pennsylvania, Dated 1822
Diameter 9¾"

Drape-molded plate with slip-trailed decoration of tulips, leaves, and splashes of green copper oxide; dated "1822". **(E)**

4.2 Plate
Eastern Pennsylvania, c. 1850
Diameter 7¾"

Drape-molded round plate of red earthenware with pattern of waves trailed in white slip, highlighted with green (copper oxide); clear lead glaze over front only; unmarked. **(C)**

4.3 Dish
Montgomery County, Pennsylvania, c. 1796
Diameter 14"

Large wheel-thrown dish with slip-trailed tulip and bird design at center, border inscription translates from the Pennsylvania German as "Good and Bad luck are our daily breakfast fare." **(E)**

National Gallery of Art, Index of American Design

4.4 Pan
Eastern Pennsylvania, c. 1790
Diameter 7"

Deep pan of red earthenware with slip-trailed concentric circles and wavy lines, clear lead glaze. **(C)**

National Gallery of Art, Index of American Design

4.5 Pitcher
Possibly Reading, Pennsylvania
c. 1840
Height 4⅞"

Wheel-thrown pitcher with decoration of spattered white slip and manganese brown spots, clear lead glaze overall. **(C)**

Nancy & Gary Stass Collection

5 | Redware: New Jersey Slip Decoration

Earthenware has a long history of manufacture in New Jersey. From the time Daniel Coxe founded a pottery at Burlington in 1685, ceramics have been a major product, due, in large part, to the extensive deposits of clay mined from Seigletown (now Finesville) down along the Delaware River to Bridgeton, and from Trenton to Elizabeth. Bricks were the crudest form of redware made from this low-grade glacial clay and were utilized until the end of the nineteenth century.

It has been suggested that the migration of redware potters to New Jersey played an important part in eventually carrying Pennsylvania styles to New England, particularly southwestern Connecticut. Due to the numerous similarities among the pottery in these regions, collectors must be aware that precise identification is not always possible.

New Jersey redware decorators, like their Pennsylvania and New England counterparts, also used distinctive slip-trailed designs. The most common of these designs is called "withering corn" by collectors and, while shared by a few Pennsylvania redware potteries, it was used primarily in southern New Jersey. The rare bird design attributed to the Matawan area and the "wave-and-blot" motif identified with the Trenton area are slip decorations which seem to be exclusive to those locations.

5.0 Plate (color plate)
Rahway Pottery
Rahway, New Jersey, c. 1800-1830
Diameter 11"

Drape-molded plate with slip-trailed inscription "Rahway Pottery" and double reverse squiggles above and below; clear lead glaze on front. **(E)**

New Jersey State Museum

**5.1 Plate
Attributed to Matawan,
  New Jersey, c. 1800-1825
Diameter 12"**

Drape-molded plate of red earthenware decorated with white slip-trailed bird in the center and wave-band above and below. **(E)**

Private Collection

**5.2 Plate
John and William Hancock, Congress Pottery
South Amboy, New Jersey
1828-1840
Diameter 9 ⅞"**

Drape-molded red earthenware plate with coggled edge, white slip-trailed inscription "Hancock/Pottery"; clear lead glaze. **(E)**

**5.3 Plate
Joseph McCully (1757-1820) or
  nephew, Joseph McCully
  (1771-1872)
Trenton, New Jersey, c. 1800-1850
Diameter 11 ⅝"**

Drape-molded red earthenware plate with white slip-trailed wavy lines alternating with bands of slip-trailed smudges. Clear lead glaze on front. Mark impressed on unglazed back "J. McCully/Trenton" in an oval. The McCullys operated their pottery until 1852. **(C)**

New Jersey State Museum

**5.4 Large Dish
Attributed to George Wolfkiel
  (active 1830-c. 1870)
Bergen County, New Jersey
c. 1840
Length 15 ⅝"; Width 12¼"**

Drape-molded red earthenware plate with white slip-trailed legend "Hard times in Jersey"; lead glaze on front. Wolfkiel, a Pennsylvania-German potter, set up a pottery about 1830 on the banks of the Hackensack River above present-day River Edge. **(E)**

Wadsworth Atheneum

5.5 Dish
Possibly Matawan, New Jersey
1800-1850
Length 16⅞"; Width 11⅝";
Height 2½"

Large drape-molded dish of red
earthenware with white slip decoration of "withering corn" between diagonal rows of wavy slip
lines, clear lead glaze overall. **(D)**

Nancy & Gary Stass Collection

6 | Redware: Shenandoah Valley Slip Decoration

One region encompassing a most active heritage of redware pottery
is that which stretches from Chambersburg, Pennsylvania, in the
north, along the Great Wagon Road or Shenandoah Valley Pike to
Harrisonburg, Virginia in the south. A southward migration of mostly
German families, particularly from Pennsylvania and Maryland,
brought craftsmen, farmers, and entrepreneurs who made and used
distinctive ceramic wares.

The most prominent family of potters in the Shenandoah Valley was
the Bell family. In Hagerstown, Maryland, Peter Bell operated a pottery as early as 1805, and by 1824 had moved south to Winchester, Virginia. Other members of the family—John, Samuel, John W., Upton,
and Solomon—manufactured redware (and stoneware) at Waynesboro, Pennsylvania, and Strasburg, Virginia.

A common decorative process used in the Shenandoah Valley was
first to coat the pieces with a fine white slip and then brush, drip, or
spatter brown, green, and occasionally, blue glazes over the white
ground; finally, applying a relatively clear (appears somewhat
yellow from iron impurities) lead glaze overall. The brightly colored effect of these glazes is distinctive to Shenandoah Valley redware.

An abundance of molded forms and sculptural shapes is another
characteristic of these Shenandoah Valley pieces. Plain, slightly
thick utilitarian redware was also produced in most of the same
shapes, but the Bells and their fellow craftsmen—Anthony W. Baecher,
the Eberly family, J.G. Schweinfurt, and others—are most popular with
collectors because of their imaginative shapes and generous use of
colored glazes.

6.0 Pitcher (color plate)
Possibly S. Bell & Sons (1882-1904)
Strasburg, Virginia (Shenandoah Valley), c. 1875-1900
Height approximately 9"

Wheel-thrown cylindrical pitcher of red earthenware, applied ear-shaped handle; white slip ground with green and brown splotches and clear lead glaze overall. **(C)**

NMAH

6.1 Bowl and Pitcher
Solomon Bell (1837-1882)
Strasburg, Virginia, c. 1860
Height, pitcher 11⅜"; Width,
    bowl 13½"

Wheel-thrown and modeled bowl and pitcher of red earthenware with characteristic white slip ground with green and brown spotted and dripped decoration and clear lead glaze overall. **(E)**

NMAH

6.2 Cuspidor
Attributed to Solomon Bell & Sons
    (1837-1882)
Strasburg, Virginia, c. 1860
Diameter 6¼"

Red earthenware cuspidor with white slip ground spotted with green and brown metallic oxides, clear lead glaze overall. **(C)**

Private Collection

6.3 Wall Pocket
Attributed to J. Eberly and
    Company (1880-1906)
Strasburg, Virginia, 1880-1900
Height 7¼"

Hanging wall pocket of red earthenware with molded decoration of roses and shells, covered with white slip ground with green and brown spots; clear lead glaze overall.

Private Collection

6.4 Preserve Jar
Morgantown, West Virginia
c. 1825
Height 10¼"

Wheel-thrown cylindrical jar of redware with white, green, and brown stylized flowers executed in slip; clear lead glaze overall. **(C-D)**

NMAH

7 | Redware: New York Slip Decoration

The majority of settlers in New York State were from New England, therefore, most of the New York redware reflects New England traditions. Recent research, however, has shed light on those potters of German heritage who moved into the Mohawk Valley, Rochester, and Buffalo areas and developed a local tradition of colorful, marbleized slip-decorated redware.

In almost every instance, redware found from this region may be dated to the nineteenth century since the area was somewhat remote and slow to be settled. Some of the Germanic craftsmen produced wares covered in white slip (engobe) and ornamented with powdered metallic oxides producing speckled greens and browns.

Other western New York potteries, like the one in West Bloomfield Township, Ontario County, produced wares with applied, swirled yellow, brown, and green slip to create a marbleized effect directly on the redware body without using engobe backgrounds. The "Nathaniel Rochester" Pottery in West Bloomfield also manufactured drape-molded redware plates with coggled or plain edges and turned bowls and pans decorated with slip-trailed linear designs closely resembling those found in Pennsylvania. These New York State plates may be distinguished by their deep profiles, rounded bottoms, and often exaggerated thickness.

An unusual type of slip-decorated redware was made in western New York at several localities, including the Lorenzo Johnson Pottery in Erie County. This mid- and late-nineteenth-century redware was covered in a light-colored slip and then decorated with brushed blue or green slips in obvious imitation of the superior blue-decorated stoneware then being produced in New York. These imitations were also being made by some redware potters in Ontario, Canada, suggesting that there may have been some interchange of workmen, or ideas, across national borders.

7.0 Jar (color plate)
Attributed to West Bloomfield Township
Ontario County, New York, c. 1820-30
Height 9⅜"

Ovoid red earthenware jar with blue and white slip decoration splashed under a clear lead glaze. The green and orange variations in the ground are due to variations in the clay in conjunction with the atmosphere in the kiln. **(E)**

Collection of Kathleen S. and George R. Hamell

7.1 Pitcher
Western New York State
(Rochester-Monroe County Region), c. 1820-1840
Height 10¼"

Bulbous red earthenware pitcher with high neck, applied strap handle, marbleized white slip with brown and green glazes **(D-E)**

Collection of Kathleen S. and George R. Hamell

7.2 Large Plate
Attributed to Huntington, Long Island, New York, 1800-1850
Diameter 13¼"

Drape-molded red earthenware plate with white slip-trailed central sun or star motif, clear lead glaze. **(D)**

Nancy & Gary Stass Collection

7.3 Jug
Lorenzo Johnson (c. 1850-1886)
Newstead Township, Erie County,
   New York, c. 1850
Height 11¾"

Wheel-thrown ovoid jar of red earthenware with mottled gray-green and tan lead glaze overall, blue slip decoration; impressed mark above flower "L.JOHNSON." The color and decoration imitate salt-glazed stoneware of the same period. **(C-D)**

Collection of Kathleen S. and George R. Hamell

7.4 Jar
Western New York State
   (Rochester-Monroe County
   Region), c. 1820-1840
Height 9¾"

Wheel-thrown red earthenware jar with decoration of bird incised into reddish-orange slip and filled with manganese (black). Figural decoration is rare in this region. **(E)**

Collection of Kathleen S. and George R. Hamell

8 | Redware: Moravian Slip Decoration

Into the wilderness that was eighteenth-century North Carolina came religious settlers, the Moravians, from Pennsylvania and Central Europe. After 1753 the town of Wachovia ("Bethabara") was established and by 1772 the central city of Salem (from the Hebrew for "peace") was ready for the major congregation. The community was completely dependent on the church, which owned all the land. In the beginning, craftsmen, including potters, were hired by the church administration; however, by the mid-nineteenth century, rigid dogma failed to protect the congregations from the enticements of a free society.

The most famous and influential of the Moravian redware potters,

Gottfried Aust (1722-88), was born in Silesia (now Czechoslovakia) and apprenticed to the potter's trade in Germany. He soon migrated to the substantial settlement at Bethlehem, Pennsylvania, where a pottery had been in operation since 1744. After a short stay in Bethlehem he left for Bethabara where he was master potter from 1755 to 1771. Later, he performed the same role in Salem (1771-88). His products included simple utilitarian forms, such as molded stove tiles, drinking vessels, and lighting devices. In his work the traditional German forms and decorative style were dominant.

Soon other craftsmen studied with Aust and their production of ceramic wares helped to supply settlements as far away as Kentucky. Slip-trailed designs in white, red brown, and green sometimes imitated those made in Bethlehem and other Pennsylvania pottery centers, but the majority of North Carolina slip patterns closely resemble their Middle-European antecedents. Floral decoration and unusual abstract lunettes, crosshatching, and sunbursts were very popular. Some later wares exhibit a strong English influence. Eventually, fancy molded redware plates, bottles, and flowerpots with colored slip overall and streaked glazes partially supplanted the taste for the more traditional work in the European style.

8.0 Plate (color plate)
Attributed to Gottfried Aust (1722-1788)
Salem, North Carolina, c. 1780
Diameter 13½"

Wheel-thrown plate decorated with floral design and concentric line border in green, brown, and red slips over a white slip ground; clear lead glaze overall. **(E)**

Old Salem Restoration

8.1 Plate
Attributed to Rudolph Christ, (1750-1833)
Salem, North Carolina, c. 1800
Diameter 10¼"

Wheel-thrown plate of red earthenware covered in dark brown slip and decorated with white, green, and red slip designs; lead glaze overall. **(E)**

Old Salem Restoration

8.2 Plate
Wachovia, North Carolina, c. 1780-1820
Diameter 15½"

Wheel-thrown red earthenware plate with flat bottom and wide, flat rim; the top covered with white slip with red and green scattered flowers and leaves; clear lead glaze overall. **(E)**

8.3 Mug
Probably Salem, North Carolina
1800-1850
Height 3⅓" (one-half pint
**   capacity)**

Wheel-thrown mug with applied handle, covered in white slip with green and purple-brown sponged spots and clear lead glaze. **(D)**

Old Salem Restoration

8.4 Preserve Pot
Attributed to Rudolf Christ,
**   (1750-1833)**
Salem, North Carolina, c. 1800
Height 4¾"

Wheel-thrown red earthenware pot having a domed lid with round finial; decorated with concentric white and brown slip bands and lead glaze overall. **(D-E)**

Old Salem Restoration

8.5 Bowl
Attributed to Rudolf Christ
**   (1750-1833)**
Salem, North Carolina, c. 1810
Height 2½"; Diameter 8⅝"

Round wheel-thrown bowl of red earthenware decorated with simple wavy and straight lines in white, brown, and green slip; clear lead glaze overall. **(D)**

Old Salem Restoration

9 | Redware: Colored Glazes

Although the slip-decorated redwares discussed in the previous chapter are sometimes quite colorful, they may be distinguished from those wares considered in this section by their dominant use of white slip, either trailed or used as a background for colored metallic glazes. The redware in this category depends solely on naturally occurring or deliberately employed oxides to give variety to the basic red background color of the clay: iron for brown, manganese for black, and copper for green. The most common clear glaze consisted of powdered red lead, sand (silica), and water, producing a glassy coating which intensified the red clay color, but left the taste for a fancier product unsatisfied.

Potters throughout the country have taxed their imaginations attempting to find easy solutions to the problem of decoration. The simplest answer has been to splash, brush, drip and otherwise "paint" the unadorned redware with metallic oxides. The basic application of a few spots of black or brown to ornament a pot may be found on wares made in New England, the Middle Atlantic States, the South, and the Midwest (to some extent).

There are regional aspects to the use of overall green, brown, black, and striking patterns of these colors, but the potters of New England are renowned for the richness of their simple color effects. Sometimes these results were caused by impurities in the lead glaze or in the clay itself, producing a mottled appearance like that found on the wares attributed to Gonic, New Hampshire. Because the copper oxide was relatively scarce, green glazes like those occurring on some Massachusetts, New Hampshire, and Maine redwares are particularly valued by collectors.

Variations in the atmosphere of the kiln were also responsible for certain color effects obtained from the use of metallic oxides. Ferric oxide, for example, will produce a yellow to brown color in an oxidation atmosphere, while in a reduction atmosphere (absence of oxygen) the same oxide will turn green. It is often difficult to determine whether these effects were achieved accidentally or intentionally, but the results are sometimes strikingly beautiful.

9.0 Jug (color plate)
Probably Gonic, New Hampshire, c. 1825
Height 5¼"

Small, ovoid jug of red earthenware with applied loop handle; green-tinted top half, brown spots, random orange spots, and lead glaze overall. **(C)**

Nancy & Gary Stass Collection

9.1 Jug
Galena, Illinois, 1850-1880
Height 9¾"; Diameter 7"

Wheel-thrown jug with tooled collar and lip, applied handle; decorated with three large "full moon"
designs in tan slip on shoulder and
clear lead glaze overall. **(C)**

National Gallery of Art, Index of
American Design

9.2 Jug
New England, 1800-1850
Height 9¾"

Wheel-thrown ovoid jug with short, flattened lip; covered with an iridescent dark green glaze. **(C)**

9.3 Jug
Probably Massachusetts, 1790-1825
Height 11½"

Wheel-thrown ovoid jug of red earthenware with applied strap handle; covered in a deep mossy-green glaze. **(C)**

9.4 Batter Jug
Eastern Pennsylvania, c. 1840
Height 8¾"; Diameter 6¾"

Wheel-thrown and modeled jug
of red earthenware, unusual applied strap handle across top and
spout, incised wavy band at shoulder, brown manganese spots with
clear lead glaze overall. **(C)**

Private Collection

**9.5 Crock
Attributed to Huntington,
  Long Island, New York
1800-1840
Height 10⅜"; Diameter 8¼"**

Wheel-thrown bulbous crock of
red earthenware, straight neck,
double incised lines around shoulder, coggled band at neck, applied handles, red-brown splotches with clear lead glaze. **(C)**

Nancy & Gary Stass Collection

**9.6 Crock
Matawan or Woodbridge,
New Jersey, 1830-1850
Height 8¼"**

Wheel-thrown ovoid crock with
neck flaring outward slightly, incised lines on shoulder, tooled
band at neck, applied "heart"
handles, brown spots under clear
lead glaze. **(B-C)**

New Jersey State Museum

**9.7 Covered Jar
Southwestern Connecticut,
  c. 1800-1825
Height 11¼"**

Wheel-thrown bulbous jar with inset lip for the cover; large spots of
dark brown oxide under a clear
lead glaze. **(B-C)**

**9.8 Covered Jar
Chesham, New Hampshire
1800-1825
Height 11"**

Wheel-thrown covered jar of red
earthenware with streaked and
speckled green glaze. **(C-D)**

NMAH

9.9 Mug
Solomon Miller
Hampton, Pennsylvania
Dated June 22, 1872
Height 3½"

Wheel-thrown red earthenware mug flaring out towards rim, applied ear-shaped handle, brown brushed spots on sides, signed and dated on the bottom. **(C)**

NMAH

9.10 Bowl
Peter Flanders
West Plymouth, New Hampshire
1807-1869
Diameter 9½"

Wheel-thrown red earthenware bowl with incised horizontal lines and dark green-tinted lead glaze. **(C)**

NMAH

9.11 Covered Pitcher
New England, 1800-1850
Height 7½"

Wheel-thrown ovoid pitcher with modeled lip, incised lines at shoulder; covered in dark green and clear lead glaze overall. **(C)**

10 | Redware: Molded and Modeled

There are many examples of redware which have been either molded or modeled by hand into ordinary utilitarian forms, but the pieces in this category are so fancifully embellished as to disguise their utilitarian function. Some are useful only as ornaments, while others depend on decoration to lift them above their more prosaic brethren. The artistic impulse of the potter to mold and model is frequently governed by the expectations of his customers.

Humorous animal and human figures were very popular with the Pennsylvania Germans. A number of potteries in this area employed modelers who crafted monkeys dressed in coat and pants (some riding elephants while drinking from a bottle), old hound dogs with fiddlers, and other silly notions in clay. A more common type of animal figurine is the seated spaniel, which was copied from English

Staffordshire earthenware examples. These figurines were popular as mantel ornaments for many years and the American potters were quick to capitalize on this increased demand.

The ease with which clay may be manipulated led some potters to create elaborate shallow relief-molded ornaments, particularly for flowerpots and pitchers. A few craftsmen like David Waring and John Nase of eastern Pennsylvania took risks with the fickle material and dared the blazing kiln to melt their fragile pierced sugar and tobacco bowls.

10.0 Figurine (color plate)
Eastern Pennsylvania, 1825-1875
Height approximately 6"

Hand-modeled of red earthenware and covered with a lead glaze, this figure of a dog sitting up and drinking from a bottle is typical of the decorative and amusing pieces made by potters in Pennsylvania. Few of these figures that survive are signed or attributable to a particular pottery. **(E)**

Courtesy of Bernard and S. Dean Levy, Inc.

10.1 Figurine
Eastern Pennsylvania, c. 1825
Height 6¾"; Width 6½"

Hand-modeled redware figurine of a seated dog with a basket in its mouth; incised details and impressed ovals on base; clear glaze overall. **(E)**

National Gallery of Art, Index of American Design

10.2 Figure
John Bell
Waynesboro, Pennsylvania, c. 1860
Height 9"

Molded red earthenware figure of a seated spaniel patterned after the English Staffordshire mantel ornaments; incised collar and leash; covered in a streaky brown and clear lead glaze. **(C)**

10.3 Figure
Attributed to Samuel Bell
Strasburg, Virginia, c. 1850
Height 6½"

Hand-modeled comic figure of red earthenware depicting a musician playing the fiddle, seated on a stump with a dog at his feet, all on a long flat oval base with double line of impressed ovals; olive-tinted lead glaze overall. **(E)**

10.4 Bottle
Salem, North Carolina, 1775-1825
Height 7 ⅞ "

Molded red earthenware bottle in the shape of a squirrel, green and brown over white slip, clear lead glaze overall. **(E)**

Old Salem Restoration

10.5 Pitcher
Solomon Bell (1837-1882)
Strasburg, Virginia, c. 1860
Height 7½"

Footed pitcher of molded red earthenware with relief design of hunting scene; brown sponged spots and clear lead glaze overall. **(C-D)**

NMAH

10.6 Dish
Jacob Taney
Nockamixon, Pennsylvania, 1790-1800
Height 1½"; Diameter 8½"

Drape-molded octagonal dish with designs of stylized flowers and leaves in low relief; dark lead glaze overall. **(D)**

10.7 Covered Bowl
Probably David Waring
Bucks County, Pennsylvania
c. 1835
Height 7"; Width 10½"

Wheel-thrown and modeled covered bowl having double walls, the outer wall carved with geometric designs; acorn and leaf finial; modeled rope handles. **(E)**

National Gallery of Art, Index of American Design.

10.8 Paperweight
Henry M. or Charles S. Spence
Adams County, Pennsylvania, 1885-1893
Height 5¼"; Width 4"

Molded rectangular-shaped plaque of red earthenware with relief portrait bust of Abraham Lincoln; made of "clay from the Gettysburg Battlefield"; scrolled border; unglazed. **(B)**

11 | Redware: Canadian

During its early years of development, Canada, like the United States, was forced to depend almost entirely on manufactured goods from abroad. The earliest known redware potter was Gabriel Lemieux, who, with the permission of the governor of New France, established his business in 1694. Like other early potteries, Lemieux's was located along the St. Charles River at Charlesburg, east of Quebec.

These early wares were comprised of the simplest functional bowls, pots, plates, and the necessary brick and tile construction materials. The Quebec forms closely resembled their French counterparts, but the copper green glazes of the French ware were unavailable or simply not used by the potters of New France. Just as the earliest American redware is known primarily from archaeological reconstructions, the Canadian examples are usually found underground. Collectors must be wary of accepting period French pieces and later English pieces as substitutes for native Canadian redwares of the eighteenth and nineteenth centuries.

It was not until the nineteenth century that Canadian redware potters began to produce more than the most common utilitarian examples. England still supplied the vast majority of ceramics used in the province, but by the mid-nineteenth century the influx of English, German, and American immigrant potters and the availability of venture capital permitted the local industries in Ontario, Quebec, and the Maritime Provinces to develop. Although the ceramic industry as a whole was growing during this period, redware production declined as stoneware became more popular. Redware potters, consequently, supplied mostly common and cheap utilitarian wares in the rural areas and some Victorian decorative vases and figurines. A few factories also produced slip-coated redware with green and blue decoration in an attempt to imitate the stoneware that was so much in demand.

11.0 Two Bowls (color plate, left)
Prince Edward Island Pottery (1880-1895)
Charlottetown, Prince Edward Island, 1880-1895
Diameter of bowl in background 12½"

Wheel-thrown utility bowls of red earthenware with distinctive looped decoration in white slip; lead glaze overall. The reconstructed example in the foreground was excavated from the site of this pottery in 1970. [A dog figurine and various kiln implements are also included.]**(C)**

Royal Ontario Museum, Canadiana Department

11.1 Bowl and Jug
Bowl: Attributed to Adam Bierenstahl Pottery, Bridgeport, Ontario
Jug: Joseph Wagner Pottery (marked), Berlin, Canada West
c. 1860-1880
Diameter, bowl 16½"; Height, jug 13¼"

Wheel-thrown bowl and jug with applied handles, both covered in white slip and decorated with flower designs in green; adapted from local stoneware decoration. **(C, each)**

Royal Ontario Museum, Canadiana Department

11.2 Bowl
Probably Dion Pottery
Quebec, Quebec Province
c. 1870-1918
Diameter 9 ⅛"

Round, wheel-thrown utility bowl
with characteristic Quebec-area
pouring spout at rim; glaze has
greenish tinge speckled with
orange. **(B)**

Royal Ontario Museum, Canadiana Department

11.3 Two Preserve Jars
Nova Scotia, c. 1870-1890
Heights 6½" and 7½"

Wheel-thrown preserve jars with
straight sides, interiors are lead-
glazed while exteriors are glazed
only on their top halves in the style
of the Maritime Provinces. **(A,
each)**

Royal Ontario Museum, Canadiana Department

11.4 Crock
John & James Richardson (active 1860-1886)
Kerwood, Southwestern Ontario, c. 1865
Height 14" (two-gallon capacity)

Wheel-thrown red earthenware crock, slightly ovoid with applied ear-
shaped handles; covered with clear lead glaze; impressed mark on
shoulder "RICHARDSONS WARE". **(C)**

11.5 Jug
The Huron Pottery, J.B. Weber (1876-1897)
Egmondville, Ontario, c. 1880
Height 16⅜"

Wheel-thrown earthenware jug covered with white slip and having a
flower decoration in cobalt blue on the shoulder; impressed mark in
rectangle "JB WEBER/HURON POTTERY/EGMONDVILLE, ONT." **(C)**

11.6 Hanging Flowerpot
Dion Pottery
Ancienne Lorette, Quebec
c. 1900
Diameter 8½"

Wheel-thrown flowerpot with
flared sides and scalloped edge
integral with separately thrown
and applied ruffled edge, integral with separately thrown and
applied ruffled saucer base;
streaked brown over white slip
and clear lead glaze overall. **(B)**

Royal Ontario Museum, Canadiana Department

11.7 Three Flowerpots
Attributed to William Eby
Conestoga, Ontario, Canada, c. 1860-1880
Height varies, approximately 4½"-5½"

Wheel-thrown redware flowerpots with integral saucers. Spattered
brown slip decorates the two outer pots; the differences in color are
related to the differences in clay body. The center pot was brushed
with green slip. Lead glaze over all pots. **(B, each)**

Royal Ontario Museum, Canadiana Department

11.8 Plaque
Henry Prescott, James Prescott & Son
Enfield, Nova Scotia, Canada, c. 1880
Height 5¾"; Width 7"

Molded high-relief plaque of red earthenware depicting "Nova
Scotia Miners"; integral frame; incised mark on reverse "Acadia Pot-
tery/Enfield N.S." **(C)**

12 | Redware: Modern Revivals

The lead glazes used on redware contributed to stoneware's eventual dominance of the ceramic container market. Vinegar, wine, and other acidic foods, such as tomatoes, leached some of the lead salts out of the glaze and, to a degree, poisoned the consumers. The potters themselves were not immune to the effects of lead. The continued handling of lead glazes became a serious occupational hazard. By 1900, traditional redware production had almost ceased except for a few potters carrying on in a family rural tradition.

After the publication of **Tulip Ware of the Pennsylvania-German Potters** in 1903 by Edwin AtLee Barber, collectors and museums competed to acquire the few remaining examples of fancy sgraffito and slip-trailed redwares. In many areas of the country an awareness of early-American craft history created a nostalgic desire to recapture the past. Interior decorators sometimes used authentic examples of antique furniture, textiles, ceramics, etc., but the demand exceeded the supply.

The dearth of old, decorated redware and the desire for its inherent charm resulted in a revival of the craft. Jacob Medinger of Schwenksville, Pennsylvania—whose father, William, had been a potter before him—produced many of the most sought after examples until his death in 1932. Mrs. Medinger and William J. McAlister, a woodcarver, helped with the sgraffito and molded wares which were often copied from the finest antique specimens, perhaps known from Barber's book.

Another fine redware manufacture was started in 1933 by the brothers Thomas and Isaac Stahl of Lehigh County, Pennsylvania, whose family genealogy included potters dating back to 1847. Lester and Barbara Breininger of Robesonia, Pennsylvania, continue the tradition of these early potters by copying famous old designs while also adapting the early techniques to patterns of their own imagination.

The South, too, has a history of revival redwares, and, while the products are not as ornate as those of eastern Pennsylvania, they are honest in the sense of handcraft and design. Ben Owen and his co-workers at the Jugtown Pottery in Moore County, North Carolina, are the best-known of these Southern potters.

12.0 Plate and Candlestick (color plate)
Lester and Barbara Breininger
Robesonia, Pennsylvania, Both 1979
Height, candlestick 4¾"; Diameter, plate 10½"

Shallow, drape-molded plate; white slip with sgraffito "vase of flowers" design splashed with green; molded baluster-shaped candlestick with brown spots; both with transparent glaze overall; signed and dated. **(A)**

Private Collection

12.1 Pitcher
Jugtown Pottery (1921-present)
Seagrove, North Carolina
c. 1930
Height 4½"

Wheel-thrown bulbous pitcher of
red earthenware with applied
ear-shaped handle and covered
in a yellow-orange glaze; impressed mark ''JUGTOWN POT-
TERY'' in circle on bottom. (See
also 21: Modern Stoneware Revivals, and 44: Southern Art Pottery.)
(A)

Private Collection

12.2 Pitcher
Jacob Medinger (working
** c. 1900-1932)**
Schwenksville, Pennsylvania
c. 1910
Height 7¼"

Wheel-thrown bulbous pitcher of
red earthenware with applied
strap handle, coggled band at
neck and shoulder, spotted
brown and green-tinted lead
glaze. **(C)**

Nancy & Gary Stass Collection

12.3 Jug
Cucklestown Pottery Works
** (Robert Anderson)**
Richmondtown Restorations,
** Staten Island, New York, c. 1970**
Height 8"

Wheel-thrown and hand-modeled red earthenware jug in the
form of a grinning head; black
glaze with white eyes and teeth,
marked on bottom ''CUCKLES-
TOWN/POTTERY/WORKS''. **(A)**

Nancy & Gary Stass Collection

12.4 Harvest Ring Jug
Teague's Pottery (c. 1935-present) Charles Boyd Craven (born 1909)
Moore County, North Carolina, 1978
Height 9⅝"

Molded and tooled ring jug; red earthenware with lead glaze; impressed mark "C.B. CRAVEN". **(A)**

12.5 Covered Bowl
Isaac S. Stahl
Powder Valley, Lehigh County,
    Pennsylvania
Dated "7-22-1940"
Height 5¼"; Diameter 4⅝"

Wheel-thrown covered bowl of redware with incised lines at waist and crimped edge on lid; covered in a mottled deep green glaze; incised mark on bottom "Made by I.S. Stahl/7-22/1940." **(B)**

Private Collection

12.6 Pitcher
Ben Owen (worked alone 1958-
    c. 1970, previously with
    Jugtown Pottery)
Moore County, North Carolina
c. 1960
Height 3¹¹⁄₁₆"

Wheel-thrown, orange-red earthenware pitcher of baluster shape with applied ear-shaped handle and clear glaze overall. Marked "MASTER/BEN OWEN/POTTER" in circle. **(A)**

Joan Watkins

13 | Stoneware: Plain Utilitarian

Traditional stoneware is generally gray in color, depending on the type of clay used. Because it vitrifies when fired to a very high temperature, stoneware becomes impervious to water and, therefore, needs no glaze to make it watertight (as is required with earthenwares). The surface of coarse stoneware, however, is very gritty or sandy to the touch. The process of salt-glazing, invented in the Rhineland by the fifteenth century, made the surface smoother. This simple, but dangerous, process occurs during the firing of the ware. When the kiln reaches its highest temperatures (about 2200 degrees F.), common salt (sodium chloride) is shoveled into ports at the top of the kiln. The sodium combines with the silica in the clay to form the glaze, while the chlorine becomes a deadly vapor. When cooled the salt glaze is hard, glassy, and transparent.

An alternative to salt-glazing is to coat surfaces with a fine brown slip before firing. The slip is a creamy mixture of dark brown, finely grained clay with water. Because much of this dark brown clay is located in the area around Albany, New York, the material is known generically as Albany slip. It covers both the inside and outside of a vessel or is used on the inside only. Usually, when only the inside of a crock or jug is coated with slip, the outside is salt-glazed.

Coarse stoneware was intended for constant daily usage, therefore, the earliest American products are known primarily from archaeological evidence. Because of their extreme rarity, examples of stoneware made prior to 1790 have not been included here. These earliest wares were, of course, based on German and English prototypes inasmuch as the first stoneware potters in America hailed from these European traditions. Inevitably, American stoneware began to assume its own character.

Because of its utilitarian purpose, the forms of coarse gray stoneware were rather limited in range: bowls, jars, jugs, mugs, pots, and chamber pots. From the eighteenth through the nineteenth centuries these forms remained relatively constant in the traditional stoneware pottery. Their contours, however, began to change slowly over time. Except for mugs, vessel shapes of the late eighteenth century are generally ovoid—widest at the shoulder just below the neck or opening and tapering gradually inward toward a rather small bottom diameter. This ovoid form prevailed with variations until c. 1840-50 when the shapes gradually became straight-sided. In large part this was due to changing technology, especially apparent in the large competitive potteries where plunger molds with straight sides were used for jars and pots. Based on this criterion, ovoid vessels can be roughly assigned to the first half of the nineteenth century while straight-sided jugs, jars, and pots are generally from the second half of the nineteenth century.

Mugs, always straight-sided, changed very little over the years, except in regard to the process of manufacture. Earlier mugs are handmade and show the marks of an individual potter. After 1850, however, mugs were increasingly made in two-part molds. A distinctive vertical mold line, usually through the middle of the handle and down the opposite side, can easily be seen.

Most utilitarian stoneware is quite plain, the severity of the surface relieved only by the occasional mark of the maker. A rich dark brown Albany slip or glassy, pebbly salt glaze over the strict shape, however, has a definite appeal to the modern eye, even if utilitarian stoneware forms are no longer used for the purposes they were originally intended to serve.

13.0 Jug (color plate)
Horace Goodwin & McCloud Webster (c. 1810-1850)
Hartford, Connecticut, 1810-1830
Height 9½", Diameter 6½"

Ovoid stoneware jug with large loop handle from neck to shoulder, multiple grooves at neck, stamped "GOODWIN / & / WEBSTER" on shoulder opposite handle, overall medium brown slip with traces of blue on mark, handle terminals, and at neck. **(A)**

Private Collection

13.1 Jug
John Gott and Amos Palmets (1848-50)
Albany, New York, 1848-50
Height 14½" (two-gallon capacity)

Salt-glazed stoneware jug with straight sides, sloping shoulder, and applied strap handle from neck to shoulder; groove below neck opening; impressed on shoulder "GOTT & PALMETS / PHOENIX POTTERY / Hudson Street / ALBANY, N.Y. / 2". **(A)**

NMAH

13.2 Jug
Paul Cushman (active 1807-1833)
Albany, New York, 1807-1825
Height 13½"

Ovoid stoneware jug with thick loop handle from neck to shoulder, thickened neck opening, overall brown slip; impressed around shoulder "PAUL CUSHMAN". Cushman's mark sometimes included the location of his pottery one-half mile west of the Albany Goal. **(C)**

NMAH

13.3 Jug
Meyer Pottery (active 1885-1962)
Atascosa (near San Antonio), Texas, 1890-1900

One-quart capacity

Straight-sided stoneware jug with small loop handle at shoulder; glazed with Leon slip used regularly by the Meyer family; color varies from dark brown near bottom to clear green at top; stamped "RONSE AND WAHLSTAB" across shoulder (San Antonio dealers in liquors, wines, and cigars). **(B)**

13.4 Jug
Branch Green (1809-1827)
Philadelphia, Pennsylvania, c. 1815
Height 14¾"

Wheel-thrown ovoid jug of salt-glazed stoneware; two-gallon capacity; impressed mark at shoulder "B.GREEN/PHILAD:" and "WINE". **(B-C)**

13-5 Jug
Midwest United States, c. 1875-1900
Height 7"

Wheel-thrown and tooled stoneware jug covered in Albany slip and incised around the side "For pure fine Whiskey/have this Jug filled at/ McGrath and Bottom's/Shelbyville, Ky." **(B)**

13.6 Jug
Ransbottom Brothers Pottery Company (1900-present, now Robinson-Ransbottom Pottery)
Roseville, Ohio, c. 1925
Height 13"

Molded stoneware jug with straight sides glazed white; straight, tapering shoulders and neck glazed in brown slip; printed in black "LEDERER BROS./PASSAIC, N.J." (retailer's name) and crown mark on side (for pottery). **(A)**

13.7 Jar
William H. Ernest
Washington, D.C., c. 1840-1880
Height 10"

Stoneware jar having straight sides and slightly rounded shoulders with thick lip, thumbnail grooves at shoulder; salt-glazed; impressed on one side "WM. H. ERNEST / WASHINGTON / D.C." **(B)**

NMAH

13.8 Covered Jar
David L. Atcheson (1819-1887), Annapolis Pottery (1841-c. 1912)
Annapolis, Parke County, Indiana, 1841-c. 1850

Height 11½"

Ovoid jar of salt-glazed stoneware with cover, distinctive outflaring neck, and handles against the shoulder. Impressed below neck "D.L.ATCHESON/ANNAPOLIS. IA." Atcheson owned the pottery with partners at various times, including Jacob Cartmill and the brothers Jacob and John Bennage. There was a tendency for individual potters to mark wares with their own names rather than a company name. **(B)**

Collection of Mr. & Mrs. Malcolm Porter

13.9 Jar with Lid
Orcutt & Crafts Pottery (active 1835-1837)
Portland, Maine, 1835-1837
Height 13⅓" (three-gallon capacity)

Ovoid jar of salt-glazed stoneware with thick, round, ear-shaped handles applied on the shoulder, vertical neck, brown slip inside; impressed on shoulder "ORCUTT & CRAFTS / PORTLAND"; inset lid with button finial and "3" impressed on top. **(B)**

NMAH

13.10 Jar
John B. Ziegler
Bellevue, Nebraksa, c. 1865
Two-gallon capacity

Cylindrical jar with slightly rounded shoulders, thickened top rim; impressed "2" below neck opening with impressed mark below in circle "J.B.ZIEGLER. / BELLEVUE." **(B)**

Nebraska State Historical Society

13.11 Jar
John Remmey III (active 1791-1831)
New York, New York, 1795-1830
Height 9⅓"

Ovoid jar of salt-glazed stoneware with standaway loop handles, two grooves below straight neck; impressed on shoulder "J.REMMEY / MANHATTAN-WELLS / NEW YORK". Several generations of the Remmey family were active as potters in New York and Philadelphia. **(C)**

NMAH

13.12 Crock
George Husher (working 1867-c. 1890)
Brazil, Clay County, Indiana, c. 1870-1880
Height 12½"

Cylindrical, salt-glazed stoneware crock with small flat rim and small handles against the body; Albany slip inside, impressed mark below rim "4/GEORGE/HUSHER." in a serrated rectangle. **(B)**

Collection of Mr. & Mrs. Melvin Davies

13.13 Preserve Jar
Possibly Farrar Pottery (1841-1927)
St. Johns, Quebec, c. 1895
Height 8¼"

Slightly ovoid jar of salt-glazed stoneware with wire clamp holding glass lid with "Farrar's Patent Self Sealing Jar 1893". Complicated devices such as this one were made to compete with glass preserve jars with gasket or clamp seals. **(A)**

NMAH

**13.14 Preserve Jar or Bottle
Smith & Day Pottery (working 1843-1849)
Norwalk, Connecticut, 1843-1849
Height 9¾"**

Cylindrical stoneware bottle with angular shoulder and narrow, tall neck; brown slip overall; impressed on side in oval "SMITH & DAY, / MANUFACTURERS, / NORWALK, CON". **(A)**

NMAH

**13.15 Preserve Jar
William Grindstaff (working c. 1870-1884)
Blount County, Tennessee, Dated 1871
Height 12"**

Wheel-thrown preserve jar of stoneware with applied "lug" handles, salt-glazed, impressed "W GRINSTAFF 1871 [with G and 7 inverted]". This potter frequently inverted the "W" and "G" in his mark. **(B)**

**13.16 Beer Bottle
Middle Atlantic States, 1850-1875
Height 8¾"**

Wheel-thrown stoneware bottle with salt glaze which has covered and burned unevenly. Unlike most of today's glass versions, bottles like this one were returnable and refillable. **(A)**

Private Collection

13.17 Flask
Unidentified Maker
United States, 19th century
Height 8"

Oval flask of salt-glazed stoneware with two flat sides and reed-
ed neck. A pocket-sized container for alcohol. **(A-B)**

NMAH

13.18 Bottle
Unidentified Maker
United States, Dated 1853
Height 10"

Cylindrical bottle of salt-glazed
stoneware with tall, sloping neck
and thickened mouth opening
highlighted with blue; impressed
on shoulder "G. VICKARY / 1853",
probably the name of the retailer
who ordered the bottle. **(A)**

NMAH

13.19 Mug
Jacob Dorris Craven (1827-1895)
Randolph County, North
**   Carolina, 1883-1895**
Height 3¼"

Cylindrical mug with applied ear-
shaped handle and series of five
thumbnail grooves near bottom;
overall brown slip; impressed "JD.
CRAVEN" near bottom of handle.
(A)

NMAH

13.20 Mug
Unidentified Maker
United States, c. 1800
Height 6½"

Cylindrical stoneware mug with ear-shaped handle at side, grooves around middle and at bottom. Although mugs were used in the home, many thousands were made for the consumption of beverages in roadside taverns.
(B)

National Gallery of Art, Index of American Design

13.21 Pitcher
Unidentified Maker
Bangor, Maine, 1850-1875
Height 10⅝"

Slightly ovoid stoneware pitcher pinched at neck with thickened top rim and two thumbnail grooves near middle; strap handle; overall brown slip; impressed on shoulder below spout "BANGOR, MAINE".
(A)

NMAH

13.22 Chamber Pot
Unidentified Maker
United States, 19th century
Diameter 8"

Ovoid chamber pot of salt-glazed stoneware with broad rim, ear-shaped handle, series of thumbnail grooves below rim, brown slip on inside; spotted surface is from impurities in clay. This ubiquitous form is difficult to date precisely.
(A)

NMAH

13.23 Cheese Strainer
United States, Early 19th century
Height 6½"

Round, flat strainer of stoneware with short sides, pierced overall with
numerous small holes; tall strap handle with cobalt blue wash; salt-
glazed overall. **(B)**

14 | Stoneware: Incised or Impressed Decoration

Decoration on stoneware was often accomplished by incising
straight or wavy lines, by impressing or stamping a design, or by the
use of a coggle wheel. Continuous incised lines around the vessel
were done with a small, sharp instrument while the piece was still on
the wheel. The coggle wheel, a small cylinder of clay or wood into
which a design has been cut, also produced continuous decoration
when mounted on a handle and pressed into the vessel as it turned
on the potter's wheel.

Designs were also created with stamps cut from a variety of materials and impressed into the damp surface one or more times. This is the
method by which the pottery's name was added to a piece.

Freehand decorations were also incised into the damp surface of
vessels, but, because this technique was time-consuming, it is rarely
encountered. Much of what survives was probably made as a gift
from the potter or on special commission. Pieces with freehand decoration are often quite valuable. Except for simple lines, the incised, impressed, and coggled decorations are usually associated with stoneware of the late eighteenth and early nineteenth centuries.

14.0 Jar (color plate)
Thomas H. Commeraw (active 1897-1899 and 1802-c. 1819)
New York, New York, 1897-c. 1815
Height 12¼"

Ovoid jar of salt-glazed stoneware with loop handles on shoulder;
series of thumbnail grooves below thickened mouth opening; impressed half-moons and tassels filled with blue on shoulder and
stamped below "COMMERAWS / STONEWARE [with "S" and "N" in-
verted] in large letters. **(D)**

NMAH

14.1 Jug
Nathan Clark & Company (1835-1846)
Mount Morris, Livingston County, New York, 1835-1846
Height 11¼"

Wheel-thrown ovoid jug of salt-glazed stoneware with incised decoration of sailing ship, highlighted with cobalt blue; impressed mark below mouth "N. CLARK & CO./MOUNT MORRIS." Clark owned several potteries along the Hudson River and Erie Canal. **(E)**

Collection of Kathleen S. and George R. Hamell

14.2 Jug
Goodale & Stedman (active 1818-1830)
Hartford, Connecticut
Dated 1822
Height 17"

Ovoid, salt-glazed stoneware jug with ribbed neck and loop handle; incised bird on front filled with blue; also incised "3GALLON" and "1822"; impressed "GOODALE & / STEDMAN / HARTFORD" near neck, and "L WATSON" (owner) five times around jug. **(E)**

NMAH

14.3 Jug
Frederick Carpenter, Edwards Pottery (1812-1827)
Charlestown, Massachusetts
1812-1827
Height 12½"

Ovoid, salt-glazed stoneware jar with long neck, loop handle, series of grooves at neck, impressed swag with tassel design below neck. Carpenter often stamped his jugs and jars with "BOSTON", where he retailed his wares. **(C-D)**

NMAH

14.5 Jar
Probably Frederick Carpenter,
  master potter at Edwards
  Pottery (1812-1827)
Charlestown, Massachusetts
1812-1827
Height 15½"

14.4 Jug
Clarkson Crolius (active
  1794-1838)
New York, New York, c. 1800-1825
Height 11"

Ovoid, salt-glazed stoneware jug with loop handle (not shown) and incised design of double leaf filled with blue; impressed mark above design "C. CROLIUS / MANUFACTORY / MANHATTAN WELLS / NEW-YORK". **(D)**

NMAH

Ovoid, salt-glazed stoneware jar with ear-shaped handles applied to the shoulder; tall, slightly flaring neck; delicately incised design on one side consists of a conventional flower with four petals; stamped "CHARLESTOWN". **(D)**

NMAH

14.6 Jar
Probably Frederick Carpenter,
  Edwards Pottery (1812-1827)
Charlestown, Massachusetts
c. 1820
Height 10½"

Ovoid stoneware jar with brown slip under salt glaze; delicately incised decoration of bird on leafy, flowered branches; narrow coggled bands around neck and shoulder; impressed "BOSTON" above decoration indicates the city in which Carpenter's wares were marketed. **(D)**

NMAH

14.7 Jar
Probably Morgan, Van Wickle,
and Green (active 1805-22)
Old Bridge, New Jersey
1805-1822
Height 10½"

Ovoid jar of salt-glazed stoneware with flat hand-holds attached at shoulder; impressed
"man-in-the moon" motif flanked
by two vertical coggle bands of
diamond-in-diamond pattern; all
three brushed with blue. **(D)**

NMAH

14.8 Jar
Francis Nolen (working
c. 1849-1854)
Cloverland, Clay County,
Indiana, 1849-1854
Height 19¾"

Elongated ovoid jar of salt-glazed
stoneware with delicately incised
decoration of four long leaves on
a branch; elaborately impressed
"7" (gallons) with "FRANCIS/
NOLEN." impressed to left. Marks
and decoration highlighted with
cobalt blue. Nolen's early training
in Pennsylvania probably contributed to his use of incised and
blue-filled decoration which is
otherwise very unusual for Indiana
stoneware. **(C)**

Indianapolis Museum of Art

14.9 Jar
W. States
Stonington, Connecticut
1824-1835
Height 15"

Slightly ovoid, salt-glazed stoneware jar with ear-shaped handles applied to the shoulders, brown slip inside; incised design of thick leaves filled with blue; "W. STATES" impressed on shoulder. **(C)**

NMAH

14.10 Crock
New York City area, c. 1810
Height 9" (two-gallon capacity)

Wheel-thrown ovoid crock of salt-glazed stoneware with detached loop handles and bold incised flower design filled with cobalt blue; unmarked. **(C)**

14.11 Cooler
Unidentified Maker
Possibly Albany, New York, 1826-1834
Height 15½"

Barrel-shaped cooler of salt-glazed stoneware with incised figure of a fish below semi-circular frame enclosing legend "H•GIN" (probably for Holland Gin), and stamped "M.TYLER&CO / ALBANY". Made for Moses Tyler and Charles Dillon. **(E)**

NMAH

14.12 Cake Pot
Thomas Warne and Joshua Letts (active 1785-1813)
South Amboy, New Jersey, c. 1807
Height 9¾"; Diameter 11¼"

Squat, salt-glazed stoneware jar with projecting scalloped handles; a coggled, serrated band of vertical rectangles around the neck; "LIBERTY FOREV" with two fingers forming horizontal "V" within stepped frame above "WARNE & LETTs 1807" on reverse; impressed, blue-filled holly leaves below "S.AMBOY.N.JERSY." **(E)**

NMAH

15 | Stoneware: Slip-trailed Decoration

Simple blue decorations are common on salt-glazed stoneware because cobalt is the only metallic oxide which can consistently withstand the high temperatures to which stoneware is fired. A small quantity of cobalt mixed with water and finely ground sand and clay forms a blue slip. When prepared to the proper creamy consistency, the slip can be trailed onto the slightly damp surface of the vessel with a small cup fitted near the bottom with a quill. The slip cup and slip are like pen and ink in the hand of a skilled decorator. The complexity of decorations possible with these tools was bounded only by the shape of the vessel and the skill and imagination of the decorator.

Slip-trailed decorations are most commonly found on stoneware made in New England (primarily Bennington, Vermont) and in New York along the Hudson River and Erie Canal. In the Hudson-Erie area, particularly, the competition for consumer markets in stoneware was quite keen. Pieces of the mid-to-late nineteenth century from this area were, as a result, often more highly decorated than stoneware made in other areas.

Birds and flowers were very popular designs. Animals and continuous scenes are encountered more rarely. A peculiar design which appears to be a bee is often found on stoneware made in Indiana and Illinois.

15.0 Jar or Crock (color plate)
William Roberts (working 1848-1888)
Binghamton, New York, c. 1850
Height 9⅝"

Slightly ovoid, salt-glazed stoneware crock with blue slip-trailed decoration of a rooster; brown slip inside; impressed mark "ROBERTS BING-
HAMPTON, N.Y." above rooster. **(C)**

NMAH

15.1 Crock
Thompson Harrington (active
as independent 1852-1874)
Lyons, New York, c. 1860s
Height 12"

Tall, straight, salt-glazed stoneware crock with sloping shoulder
and tall rim, applied handles on
shoulder; decorated with blue slip
trailed in pattern of eight-pointed
feathered star with a face in the
center, large "2" above; impressed mark below rim "T. HAR-
RINGTON / LYONS". **(D)**

Private Collection

15.2 Jar
Unidentified Maker
New Jersey or New York
1775-1800
Height 10¼"

Ovoid jar of salt-glazed stoneware with two loop handles applied near wide rim; blue slip-
trailed decoration of multiple
"watchspring" patterns on side
and below handles. This pattern
was used at potteries in New York
and in Ringoes and Cheesequake,
New Jersey during the same period. Attributing definite origins for
these pieces is often difficult. **(D)**

NMAH

15.3 Crock
Barnabas Edmands & Co.
Charlestown, Massachusetts
c. 1860
Height 10½" (three-gallon
capacity)

Straight-sided, salt-glazed stoneware crock with thick rim, applied
handles near rim, blue slip-trailed
decoration of spotted bird on
leafy branch with flower bud,
brown slip inside; impressed mark
below rim "EDMANDS & CO. / 3".
(C-D)

NMAH

15.4 Crock
Unidentified Maker
Probably New York State, Mid-19th century
Height 11"

Cylindrical stoneware crock; salt glaze with blue trailed decoration of
stylized hollyhocks; thick rim, applied handles near rim; brown slip inside; impressed "4" (four-gallon capacity). **(C)**

15.5 Crock
Unidentified Maker
Illinois or Indiana, 1860-1880
Height 9¾"

Cylindrical crock of salt-glazed
stoneware with thick rim and applied handles near rim; decorated with trailed blue slip forming
a stylized "2" and wide column of
four continuous figure eights with
a tail; brown slip inside. **(A)**

Private Collection

15.6 Jug
**Probably Noah White (1835,
  successors through 1910)
Utica, New York, 1870s
Height 11½"**

Salt-glazed stoneware jug with
straight sides, sloping shoulder,
thickened opening, and large
loop handle; decorated on front
with trailed blue slip design of
stylized bird on a simple branch;
impressed mark on shoulder
"Babcock, Litner & Co.,/Druggists
& Grocers,/Little Falls, N.Y." **(B)**

Private Collection

15.7 Jug
**Ballard & Brothers
Burlington, Vermont, Mid-19th century
Height 11½"**

Straight-sided, salt-glazed stoneware jug with thick opening and loop
handle; trailed blue slip decoration of flower with five petals and many
decorative leaves; mark impressed above decoration "BALLARD &
BROTHERS / BURLINGTON, VT." **(B)**

15.8 Jug
**J. Fisher, Lyons Stoneware Works (c. 1882-1902)
Lyons, New York, c. 1890
Height 13½"**

Wheel-thrown and tooled stoneware jug with retailer's name "P.F.
Rauber & Bro./Rochester, N.Y." trailed on the side in cobalt blue slip;
impressed "J. FISHER/LYONS, N.Y." **(A)**

15.9 Cooler
**Julius and Edward Norton (active
  1850-1859)
Bennington, Vermont, 1850-1859
Height 24"**

Barrel-shaped cooler of salt-
glazed stoneware with elaborate,
continuous scene in blue trailed
slip depicting deer, eagle, and
lion in a landscape around the
middle with multiple blue-filled
grooves above and below; two
bung holes; impressed mark
above scene "J. & E. NORTON /
BENNINGTON VT." **(E)**

NMAH

16 | Stoneware: Brush-painted Decoration

While blue slip-trailed decorations were popular in the Northeast, brushed or painted cobalt blue decoration is more commonly encountered in the Middle Atlantic States, western Pennsylvania, and Ohio. Again, a slip was prepared of cobalt blue and finely ground sand and clay in combination with water. Decorations were executed with a finger, brush, or other flat applicator. Some of the very best brushed blue decoration was produced in potteries in the lower Delaware River Valley, especially in the Philadelphia area. Clusters of leaves and simple flowers, especially tulips and fuchsia, are often found.

In the area of New Geneva, Pennsylvania, several potters brushed brown slip onto a tan or buff-colored stoneware. The decorations of flowers, bands, and swags which were used are very similar to designs found on blue brush-decorated stoneware.

16.0 Jug (color plate)
O.F. Baker & Company
Milwaukee, Wisconsin, Mid-19th century
Height 14" (two-gallon capacity)

Ovoid, salt-glazed stoneware jug with loop handle and decoration brushed with blue depicting a bold tulip with many leaves; impressed mark also brushed with blue below neck "O F BAKER & CO / MILWAUKEE WIS" and blue painted "2". **(C)**

Private Collection

16.1 Poultry Fountain
William Henry (1823-1859)
Philadelphia, Pennsylvania, c. 1850
Height 8"

Wheel-thrown and modeled salt-glazed stoneware shaped as a jug with an applied reservoir for water on one side with large opening; brushed cobalt blue leaf decoration and impressed mark "HENRY/ PHILA". **(B)**

16.2 Jar
Richard C. Remmey
  (1859-c. 1900)
Philadelphia, Pennsylvania
c. 1860
Height 10¾"

Ovoid jar of salt-glazed stoneware with tall neck; ribbed loop handles on shoulder; brushed blue decoration of large tulip with long stem and many leaves; blue at handle terminals; "1½" impressed in circle on shoulder; impressed mark "R.C.R. / PHILA". Sev-

eral generations of the Remmey family made stoneware in New York and Philadelphia. **(B)**

NMAH

16.3 Jar
M. & B. Miller
Newport, Pennsylvania
Mid-19th century
Five-gallon capacity

Slightly ovoid, salt-glazed stoneware jar with wide mouth, flattened rim, handles applied at shoulder; blue painted decoration of two large palm leaves with single fuchsia beneath and trailing vines; impressed mark below rim "M. & B. MILLER / NEWPORT, PA" and "5". **(B)**

NMAH

16.4 Crock
Sipe, Nichols & Company (1875-1877)
Williamsport, Pennsylvania, 1875-1877
Height 11¾"; Diameter 11"

Wheel-thrown gray stoneware crock of three-gallon capacity with applied handles, brushed cobalt blue decoration of grapes and leaves; impressed mark "SIPE, NICHOLS & CO./Williamsport, Pa." **(C)**

16.5 Jar
Thomas G. Boone (active
** c. 1836-1839)**
Poughkeepsie, New York
c. 1836-1839
Height 11" (two-gallon capacity)

Ovoid jar of salt-glazed stoneware with tall neck and handles applied near rim; blue brushed decoration of simple, conventional leaf above a large painted "2"; impressed mark near rim "T.G. BOONE&C. / PO'KEEPSIE N Y". **(B)**

NMAH

16.6 Jar
J. Swank & Company (1865-1900)
Johnstown, Pennsylvania
1865-1875
Height 11¾"

Slightly ovoid, salt-glazed stone-ware jar with wide mouth, applied loop handles at shoulder; decorated with painted blue tulips with long stems and many leaves repeated around the sides; blue handles; impressed mark under one handle "J SWANK & CO / JOHNSTOWN, PA." **(B)**

NMAH

16.7 Preserve Jar
Possibly Dillon Brothers Pottery
Irontown, Ohio, c. 1870
Height 6"

Cylindrical stoneware preserve jar with salt glaze and three horizontal stripes brushed in blue. This type of decoration is also associated with south-central Pennsylvania. **(B)**

National Gallery of Art, Index of American Design

16.8 Crock
John Bell (working 1833-1880)
Waynesboro, Pennsylvania, c. 1845
Height 13"; Diameter 11" (three-gallon capacity)

Wheel-thrown ovoid crock of salt-glazed stoneware with applied handles; decorated around shoulder with brushed flower and leaf design in cobalt blue; impressed mark "JOHN BELL/WAYNESBORO". **(D)**

16.9 Jar
Solomon Bell (active 1834-1882)
Strasburg, Virginia, c. 1840
Height 15¼" (four-gallon capacity)

Large ovoid jar of salt-glazed stoneware with square lip, ribbed handles applied on shoulder; brushed blue decoration of repeating pendant tulips and leaves below rim; impressed mark "SOLOMON BELL / STRASBURG, VA". **(C-D)**

16.10 Churn
Unidentified Maker
Western Pennsylvania
Mid-19th century
Height 18"

Salt-glazed stoneware churn with applied flat handles; brushed blue decoration of cloaked figure with rifle standing between two trees; impressed "6" in a circle near rim. **(D)**

National Gallery of Art, Index of American Design

16.11 Covered Butter Crock
Unidentified Maker
Delaware River Valley or Virginia, c. 1850-1890
Height 5½", Diameter 9"

Cylindrical butter crock with applied handles and flat, disc-shaped lid with handle; both decorated with brushed blue leaves in repeating pattern. **(B-C)**

16.12 Pitcher
Benedict Milburn, potter for
**   H.C. Smith (active 1825-41)**
Alexandria, Virginia, 1825-1841
Height 11"

Salt-glazed stoneware pitcher of bulbous body with tall, straight neck and pinched spout; large applied loop handle; blue painted decoration of chain band around top with narrow leaf band below and wide band of conventional flowers and leaves around body; marks impressed below spout "H.C.SMITH/ALEX.^{A}/D.C." and "1½". **(C-D)**

NMAH

16.13 Three Pitchers
Unidentified Makers
New Geneva - Greensboro, Pennsylvania, c. 1875
Height, tallest 9³⁄₁₆", Height, smallest 2¼"

Buff-colored stoneware with brushed brown slip decorations of tulips and meandering vines and leaves; swags from the top rims. This type of ware seems to be peculiar to the New Geneva-Greensboro area of Pennsylvania. **(C-D, each)**

Private Collection

16.14 Flowerpot
New Geneva-Greensboro area, Pennsylvania, 1850-1900
Height 8¼"

Wheel-thrown flowerpot of reddish-tan stoneware with attached saucer; decorated with flowers and vines hand-painted in dark brown Albany slip; unmarked. **(B)**

16.15 Spittoon
Eastern Ohio area, c. 1875
Height 4½"

Wheel-thrown stoneware spittoon with straight sides and sloping, applied top; brushed cobalt blue line decoration; unmarked. **(A)**

16.16 Coin Bank
Possibly New York State, c. 1835
Height 5½"

Wheel-thrown ovoid bank of salt-glazed stoneware with "button" finial on top and coin slot cut into shoulder; decorated with floral sprays brushed on with cobalt blue; unmarked. **(C)**

17 | Stoneware: Stenciled Decoration

In the counties of Washington, Greene, and Fayette in southwestern Pennsylvania, blue decoration on gray stoneware was often executed with stencils, either exclusively or in combination with brush-painted or slip-trailed designs. Between c. 1850 and c. 1900 a large stoneware industry flourished in this area. While decorating with stencils was not restricted to these counties (examples also survive from Indiana), most stencil-decorated stoneware found today is attributed to this area.

Stenciled designs included a small variety of flowers such as tulips and roses; geometric patterns such as spirals, stars, diamonds, and circles; the patriotic American eagle; birds; fruits such as pears; and miscellaneous flourishes, especially surrounding capacity numbers. Hand-painted plain bands, meander leaf bands, some generalized flowers and, very rarely, small vignettes occur in combination with stenciling.

Manufacturers also stenciled their company names on vessels. The names of James Hamilton and Co., and Hamilton and Jones, of Greensboro, are found more often on jugs and crocks than other makers, probably because both companies were in business for a number of years. In some cases the name stenciled on a vessel is that of a retailer rather than a manufacturer.

17.0 Jar (color plate)
James Hamilton & Company (active 1844-c. 1890)
Greensboro, Pennsylvania, c. 1870-1890
Three-gallon capacity

Cylindrical jar of salt-glazed stoneware with rounded shoulders, thick rim, and handles applied at shoulders; wide blue bands around top with blue stenciled decoration of scrolled leaf patterns on the front; the number "3" and company name "James Hamilton & Co./Greensboro. Pa." **(C)**

NMAH

17.1 Jar
James Hamilton & Company
(active 1844-c. 1890)
Greensboro, Pennsylvania
c. 1870-1890
Four-gallon capacity

Cylindrical stoneware jar similar to 17.0; made for "H.J. MILLER & CO./QUEENSWARE &C./ALEXANDRIA. VA." Pottery with both maker's and retailer's names provides a valuable document of trade relationships. **(C)**

NMAH

17.2 Large Preserve Jar
Greensboro-New Geneva area, Pennsylvania, c. 1870
Height 12¼"

Wheel-thrown, two-gallon preserve jar of salt-glazed stoneware with blue stenciled underglaze inscription, "R. SHRUM/Greensburgh./Pa./ 2". Reuben Shrum was a grocer for whom the jar was made at an unidentified pottery. **(B)**

17.3 Preserve Jar
A.P. Donaghho (1874-1900)
Parkersburg, West Virginia, c. 1880
Height 5⅝"; Diameter 4¾"

Tapered cylindrical jar of salt-glazed stoneware, wheel-thrown with prominent ridge at rim; on the side a stenciled mark in cobalt blue "A.P. Donaghho,/Parkersburg, W. Va." **(A)**

17.4 Preserve Jar
A. Conrad
New Geneva, Pennsylvania, c. 1875
Height 8"

Wheel-thrown and tooled cylindrical jar with lip, stencil-decorated in cobalt blue with floral scrolls and "A. CONRAD/NEW GENEVA/PA." **(B)**

17.5 Crock
Somerset Potters Works (active c. 1866-1909)
Somerset, Massachusetts, c. 1870
Height 9½" (two-gallon capacity)

Wheel-thrown and tooled cylindrical stoneware crock with applied
handles and stenciled cobalt blue decoration of two hands shaking in
greeting; impressed mark "SOMERSET/POTTERS WORKS/2". **(B)**

17.6 Crock
Thomas F. Reppert (c. 1884-1890)
Greensboro, Pennsylvania, c. 1885
Height 13⅛"; Diameter 9½" (three-gallon capacity)

Wheel-thrown cylindrical crock of salt-glazed stoneware with applied
handles; decoration of stenciled American eagle with ".T.F. REPPERT/
GREENSBORO/PA." in cobalt blue. **(C)**

17.7 Crock
Western Stoneware Company (1906-present)
Monmouth, Illinois, c. 1910
Height 9½" (two-gallon capacity)

Molded cylindrical crock of buff stoneware covered with white slip
and having a stenciled maple leaf and mark "2/WESTERN/STONEWARE
CO./MONMOUTH, ILL." in cobalt blue. **(A)**

17.8 Jug
Hamilton & Jones (active
** c. 1870-1890)**
Greensboro, Pennsylvania
c. 1875
Height 18"

Slightly ovoid jug of salt-glazed
stoneware with small straight
neck; blue stenciled decoration
of tulips, roses, and scrolls with
"HAMILTON & JONES/MANUFAC-
TURERS/GREENSBORO./PA" and
the capacity number "3". **(B-C)**

Private Collection

17.9 Jug
William R. Torbert and George S.
Baker (active 1859-c. 1900)
Brazil, Clay County, Indiana
c. 1880-1890
Height 11½"

Salt-glazed stoneware jug with
two handles; stenciled capacity
number "8" (gallons) within a
wreath and flanked by the letters
"O" and "C"; impressed "TORBERT
& BAKER" below mouth. **(B)**

Collection of Mr. & Mrs. Melvin
Davies

17.10 Jug
Oletha Pottery
Limestone County, Texas, c. 1890
Height 18"

Wheel-thrown and tooled stoneware jug with two handles, salt-glazed
and stenciled in cobalt blue "WOOTEN WELL CO./WOOTEN WELLS/
TEX". **(B)**

17.11 Jug
F.T. Wright & Son (1855-1868)
Taunton, Massachusetts, c. 1865
Height 14½"

Wheel-thrown jug of salt-glazed stoneware with tiger and round win-
dow design stenciled on the side in cobalt blue; impressed "F.T.
WRIGHT & SON/STONEWARE/TAUNTON, MASS." near top. **(B)**

17.12 Pitcher
Williams & Reppert
Greensboro, Pennsylvania
c. 1875
Height 11½"

Salt-glazed stoneware pitcher
with slightly ovoid body, tall concave neck, barely pinched spout,
and long loop handle; brushed
blue dashes, plain and squiggle
bands with stenciled leaf sprigs,
"WILLIAMS & REPPERT" above and
"GREENSBORO, PA." below. **(C)**

NMAH

17.13 Pitcher
James Hamilton & Company (c. 1852-1880)
Greensboro, Pennsylvania, c. 1870
Height 11 ⅞"; Diameter 8" (two-gallon capacity)

Wheel-thrown pitcher of salt-glazed stoneware; baluster shape with applied handle; mark stenciled in cobalt blue on side "2/JAS. HAMIL-TON/& CO./GREENSBORO./PA." **(C)**

17.14 Water Cooler
Red Wing/Union Stoneware
   Company (1906-1930)
Red Wing, Minnesota
1910-1920
Two-gallon capacity

Heavy, molded stoneware with stenciled decoration in red and blue; lid missing. Red Wing, Minnesota, was home for several large stoneware potteries from the 1870s through the 1960s. **(B)**

Courtesy of Lyndon C. Viel

18 | Stoneware: Alkaline Glazes

While the salt-glazing process was used extensively in North America, varieties of the alkaline glaze were popular in the southeastern United States. Exactly how this glazing technique was introduced to the South is still something of a mystery, for the only other area of the world where alkaline glazes were used to any extent was China. The alkaline, or sand-and-ash glaze, was usually made by mixing wood ashes with finely ground sand or sandy clay. Some potters eliminated the wood ashes and used raw lime instead. Vessels were dipped in the glaze prior to firing and while the clay was still somewhat damp.

The amount of iron present in the glaze and the atmosphere in the kiln during firing dramatically affected the final color. Tan, brown, and near-black colors are the result of different amounts of iron in an oxygen-rich (oxidation) kiln. Varying shades of green, from pale celadon to dark olive, are achieved in an oxygen-free (reduction) kiln.

Decoration, when it occurs, is usually in the form of incised straight or wavy lines. In the area of Edgefield County, North Carolina, some of the finest glazes were often used in combination with decorations of white slip trailed onto the surface. Alkaline-glazed Southern stoneware is rarely marked.

18.0 Jug (color plate)
"VCM"
Southeastern United States, probably North Carolina, 1875-1900
Height 10⅛"

Cylindrical stoneware jug with rounded shoulders, small vertical neck; small loop handle on shoulder has impressed rectangular mark with raised initials "VCM". Drippy alkaline glaze varies from a medium celadon-green to dark olive green. **(B)**

Private Collection

18.1 Jug
Elstork Pottery
Georgia, 19th century
Height 13"

Cylindrical stoneware jug with rounded shoulders, straight neck, and loop handle; covered in a deep olive-green and brown glaze. **(B)**

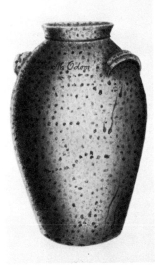

18.2 Jar
M.M. Odom and Robert Turnlee
(1859-1860)
Knox Hill, Florida, c. 1860
Height 14½"

Ovoid jar with straight neck; grooved, crescent-shaped handles applied to the shoulders and olive-green spots on the stoneware body; "M M Odom" incised on one side between the handles. **(C)**

National Gallery of Art, Index of American Design

18.3 Jar
Unidentified Maker
Southeastern United States
Second half of the 19th century
Height 16"

Slightly ovoid stoneware jar with thickened top rim and ear-shaped horizontal handles at the shoulder; lightly covered in a streaky white glaze. White effects produced by alkaline glazes are usually the result of a reduction atmosphere in the kiln or the application of white slip for decoration. **(B)**

Private Collection

18.4 Crock
J.C. Lambert
Denton County, Texas, c. 1860
Height 13"; Diameter 7"

Wheel-thrown ovoid crock of stoneware with applied handles, covered overall in an olive-green alkaline glaze; impressed "J.C. LAMBERT" and "4" (gallons) on shoulder. **(B-C)**

18.5 Churn
Unidentified Maker
Possibly North Carolina
Second half of the 19th century
Height 18½"

Cylindrical stoneware churn with vertical collar; sloping shoulders with loop handle on one side and horizontal hand-hold on the other; streaky, dark olive-green glaze. **(B)**

Private Collection

18.6 Pitcher
Unidentified Maker
Edgefield County, South Carolina
Mid-19th century
Height 5¼"

Bulbous stoneware pitcher with tall, concave neck; exaggerated pinched spout and ear-shaped handle; alkaline glaze; simple flower with leafy stem executed in white slip. Stoneware with white slip decoration on alkaline glaze is usually attributed to the Edgefield County area prior to the Civil War. **(D)**

Museum of Early Southern Decorative Arts

18.7 Ring Bottle
Unidentified Maker
Southeastern United States
Second half of the 19th century
Height 10¼"

Stoneware bottle in the shape of a circle with small spout; glossy, streaky brown glaze. **(B)**

Private Collection

---

19 | Stoneware: Molded and Modeled

In addition to the standard utilitarian wares produced in traditional stoneware potteries, potters also made articles which mirrored their desires and the desires of their customers for elaborate decoration, popular or eccentric cultural expression, or imitation of forms and designs made in more sophisticated materials.

Because clay is a malleable medium, three-dimensional decorations were made in a variety of ways. Relief designs on vessels were produced with small molds. These molds, usually of a fine-grained clay, were made by taking a direct impression from an article produced by another craftsman (cast iron trivets, for example, were occasionally the original model) or modeled by the potter. After the impression was taken and the mold thoroughly dried, it was fired to make it more permanent. The decoration on the vessel was accomplished by pressing the small mold into the surface, or, as was more commonly the method, by pressing extra clay into the wet mold and applying the small sprigs of molded clay onto the surface. Decorative handles were often made by this latter process.

Full-round decorations were also made and applied to the surface of vessels. These were modeled after a number of plants and animals, including flowers, such as roses; branches and vines; insects; reptiles, such as frogs and snakes; and various small animals. Full-round applications to pottery vessels are not very common. The Kirkpatrick brothers were perhaps the best practitioners at their pottery in Anna, Illinois (1859-1894). Their jugs—covered with snakes, frogs, spiders, and the like—are masterpieces of bizarre cultural expression in common stoneware.

Free-standing figures were often made from molds. The most common of these products were figures based on prototypes made of other materials. Stoneware dogs patterned after the popular English Staffordshire spaniels in creamware and pearl ware are most prevalent. Stately lions modeled after the mammoth stone variety are also known.

The fashionable concern for naturalism in the mid-nineteenth century is evident in the many flowerpots, pitchers, and vases modeled to imitate tree bark or vines and ivy. These are usually covered in Albany slip, often with salt glaze over the slip, which makes the surface dark and glossy. Straight-sided flowerpots, or jardinieres, were often made as a sideline in potteries specializing in sewer, or drainage, pipe. Short sections of sewer pipe (made with mechanical extruders) were easily adapted as flowerpots by closing off one end and decorating the outside.

Sewer pipe is a coarse red brown stoneware. Pipes were used in sanitary systems as well as for drainage of flooded fields. Numerous drainage pipes were manufactured during the second half of the nineteenth century when many swampy areas of land were converted to agricultural usage. In addition to jardinieres, employees in sewer pipe factories also made molded figures and other small objects as a sideline activity.

In addition to applied decorations and figures, this category also includes odd-shaped vessels. Bottles and flasks, for example, were sometimes molded into human or animal forms. An excellent example of this variety would be the small flasks in the shape of pigs produced at the Anna Pottery in southern Illinois between 1870 and 1895. The so-called Toby pitchers and mugs are also part of this phenomenon. These were molded in low relief in the form of a fat man, often holding a mug or pitcher of beer in one hand, and wearing a hat which forms the top edge. The handle is usually attached to his back.

Perhaps the most bizarre examples of molded and modeled wares are the jugs made in the form of a face. While there are isolated examples of this form made in Connecticut and Philadelphia, the practice is largely associated with the Southern alkaline-glazed tradition, particularly in North Carolina and Georgia. Often called "grotesque" jugs, they have applied noses, lips, ears, and eyelids of the same ash-glazed stoneware as the jug, but with eyeballs and teeth made of white clay or broken bits of white crockery. These jugs have been made by both black and white potters, although the features have a distinctively Negroid appearance. While it is tempting to speculate whether these jugs are a unique form of black cultural expression, the production of vessels in animal and human forms is rooted primarily in English ceramic traditions, which strongly influenced stoneware manufacture in the South.

19.0 Jug (color plate)
C. & W. Kirkpatrick, Anna Pottery (1859-1894)
Anna, Illinois, Dated 1876
Height 9 ⅞ "

Bulbous stoneware jug with applied snakes and the bottom halves of male figures; salt glaze with cobalt blue; incised legend refers to the Whiskey Scandal of President Grant's administration. The Kirkpatricks made this jug for their display at the Philadelphia Centennial and for presentation to the Smithsonian Institution afterwards. **(E)**

NMAH

19.1 Jug
Cheever Meaders (c. 1887-1976)
Cleveland, Georgia, 1967
Height 8½"

Thick facial features are added to an otherwise plain, wheel-thrown jug. The eyes and teeth are made from broken bits of white china. Lanier Meaders continues to produce "ugly" jugs at his pottery in Cleveland, Ga. **(B)**

NMAH

19.2 Jug
Unidentified Maker
Bath, South Carolina, c. 1850
Height 5"

This alkaline-glazed stoneware face jug has eyes and teeth of white kaolin. Although many of these were made by black potters (particularly around Edgefield County), the tradition in America has been traced to England during the Roman period of occupation. **(D)**

NMAH

19.3 Jar
Unidentified Maker
Charlestown, Massachusetts
c. 1850
Height 8 ⅛ "

Slightly ovoid stoneware jar with rounded rim and fat handles applied on shoulder; deeply incised line around shoulder; molded and applied rose with leaves below; the name "CHARLESTOWN" impressed between the handles. **(B-C)**

NMAH

19.4 Preserve Jar
Unidentified Maker
Peoria, Illinois
Late 19th century
Height approximately 8"

Molded stoneware preserve jar with glossy brown glaze (metal sealing lid missing). Stoneware jars were too heavy to compete successfully against glass preserve jars during the second half of the 19th century and, consequently, are much more rare. **(A)**

National Gallery of Art, Index of American Design

19.5 Crock
Weir Pottery Company (active c. 1885-1906)
Monmouth, Illinois, c. 1900
Height 5⅓"; Diameter 6⅛ "

Molded cylindrical stoneware crock with elaborate banded design and circular medallion marked "H.J. HEINZ C⁰./KEYSTONE/PICKLING & PRESERVING/WORKS/PITTSBURG, U.S.A." **(A-B)**

19.6 Pitcher
Attributed to Justus Morton, while
    working for Nathan Clark
    & Company
Lyons, Wayne County,
    New York, c. 1840-50
Height 8½"

Molded stoneware pitcher with
sprigged decoration of swags
and nosegays, the whole covered
with Albany slip. Morton had a
pottery in Brantford, Ontario,
Canada during the 1850s. **(C)**

Collection of Kathleen S. and
George R. Hamell

19.7 Toby Pitcher
Attributed to Charles Wingender
    & Brother (active 1890-1954)
Haddonfield, New Jersey
1895-1910
Height 7 ⅛"

This charming Toby pitcher was
molded and then finished with
hand-incised details. The salt-
glazed stoneware has been highlighted with cobalt blue. Some-
time after their arrival in America
from Germany, the Wingenders
settled in Haddonfield and practiced traditional pottery-making
into the twentieth century. **(D)**

NMAH

19.8 Pitcher
William Lyle, Rochester Sewer Pipe Company (1888-1901)
Rochester, New York, Dated 1888
Height 7 ⅛"

A slightly ovoid, coarse stoneware pitcher modeled to imitate a section of a tree trunk and covered with a dark brown metallic glaze. The
molded and applied ornament shows a man in colonial costume
seated on a barrel. Mr. Lyle was foreman of the Rochester Sewer Pipe
Company at the time he made this pitcher for his wife. **(C)**

19.9 Pitcher
White's Pottery (1839-1910)
Utica, New York, c. 1900
Height 8½"

Molded ovoid pitcher of stoneware with tree bark design and oval reserves with busts of Benjamin Franklin; covered in white slip with cobalt blue details; unmarked. **(B)**

19.10 Pitcher
North Star Stoneware Company (active 1892-1897)
Red Wing, Minnesota, 1892-97
Height 9¼"

Molded cylindrical pitcher of stoneware with low relief decorations of grape clusters and leaves on a basket-weave ground; zig-zag bands at top and bottom; covered with a dark brown glaze and marked on the bottom with a raised star. Millions of molded mugs and pitchers with a wide variety of low relief patterns were made into the twentieth century at many potteries in North America. **(A)**

19.11 Pitcher
Western Stoneware Company (1906-present)
Monmouth, Illinois, 1910-1930
Height 6"

Molded stoneware pitcher with busts of Indians in low relief highlighted in cobalt blue on a white ground; cobalt blue handle. Mugs and pitchers in this pattern are referred to as "Old Sleepy Eye" because they were made originally as advertising souvenirs for the Sleepy Eye (Minnesota) Flour Mill. Old Sleepy Eye was a Sioux chieftain. **(B)**

19.12 Flask
C. & W. Kirkpatrick, Anna Pottery (1859-1894)
Anna, Illinois, Dated 1874
Length 8"

This flask was made by throwing a cylinder, then modeling it into the shape of a pig and adding the details of feet, ears, and so forth. While this example is covered with a brown slip, salt glazes were also common. The Kirkpatricks began making pig-shaped flasks in the late 1860s and continued through at least 1893. **(E)**

Nancy & Gary Stass Collection

19.13 Figure
Unidentified Maker
United States, probably Ohio
Late 19th to early 20th century
Length 11½"

Coarse stoneware usually intended for sewer tile production was
used to make this figure of a lion;
molded, but with hand-incised
details, and covered with an iridescent brown glaze. Many nov-
elties were made by potters working in sewer tile factories in the
Midwest. **(B)**

Private Collection

19.14 Figure
Attributed to the Anna Pottery (active 1859-1894)
Anna, Illinois, 1870-1890
Height 21½"

Molded stoneware figure of a spaniel with details finished by hand,
covered with creamy slip and cobalt blue highlights. Many potteries in
the East and Midwest made figures of seated spaniels in imitation of
the Staffordshire earthenware figures so popular during the nineteenth
century as mantel ornaments. **(B-C)**

19.15 Doorstop
Ohio, 1850-1900
Height 6¼"

Molded stoneware figure of reclining lion on flat plinth with touches of
cobalt blue on mane and tail; unmarked. **(B-C)**

19.16 Cooler
Hastings & Belding (active
  1850-1854)
Ashfield, Massachusetts
1850-1854
Height 13¾"

This cooler has the usual barrel
shape with hoops imitated
around the body. The molded
and applied figure of George
Washington is flanked by painted
blue flowers. The mold for Washington's figure was taken from a
cast-iron stove ornament. **(E)**

NMAH

19.17 Flowerpot
S.L. Pewtress & Company (active in the 1860s)
New Haven, Connecticut
1867-1868
Height 8¾"

Stoneware molded in the form of a tree trunk with ivy growing around it; marked "S.L. PEWTRESS & CO/ NEW HAVEN CONN". The pot is covered on the outside with brown slip. Many potteries made garden crockery during the second half of the nineteenth century. **(B)**

NMAH

19.18 Coin Bank
Eastern Ohio, c. 1850
Height 4½"

Wheel-thrown and modeled bank of stoneware, dome-shaped with twisted handle at top, covered entirely with Albany slip; flat coin slot cut in front. **(B)**

19.19 Beer Bottle
Glasgow Pottery of John Moses & Company (active 1863-1895; with sons 1895-1905)
Trenton, New Jersey, 1875-1900
Height 10¼"

Molded stoneware bottle covered in white "Bristol" slip with brown glaze at top; elaborate black printed label for "The Christian Moerlein Brewing Co., Cincinnati", "Old Jug Lager"; impressed oval mark of the Glasgow Pottery on bottom. **(A)**

19.20 Stein
White's Pottery (1839-1907)
Utica, New York, 1901
Height 7"

Molded stoneware stein in buffalo design for the Pan American Exposition of 1901; metal lid; marked "White's Pottery/Utica, N.Y." **(A-B)**

20 | Stoneware: Canadian

Stoneware was not produced in Canada until 1840 or 1841 when a pottery was begun at St. Johns, Quebec, more than a century after the first stoneware was made in the colonial United States. Because the necessary clays were not found naturally in Canada, they were imported from the major stoneware clay beds in New Jersey. Canadian stoneware potteries, therefore, were established along major waterways to take advantage of this inexpensive method of transportation, as was the case in New York State and New England also.

In addition to the clay, the capital and expertise necessary to create stoneware factories also came from the United States. The shapes, technology, glazes, etc., are all similar to those employed by the generations of potters working in the United States, well after a distinctively American character in stoneware had emerged. Many of the early Canadian stoneware potters came from established potteries in New York and New England. Justin Norton, for example, established a pottery in Brantford about 1849 after working for several years for the Clark Pottery in Lyons, New York. The earliest St. Johns potter, Moses Farrar, hailed from a family of potters in Fairfax, Vermont.

The stoneware business in Canada followed much the same history as the United States potteries of the period, with the major portion of container production concentrated in the years before 1880. Afterwards, cheaper glass and metal containers claimed the consumer markets previously enjoyed by stoneware. Some small container-producing potteries remained in business until the early twentieth century. For the most part, however, those large factories which continued operating well into this century did so because they diversified their operations to include sanitary and chemical stoneware, as well as molded and slip-cast tablewares.

Because of the close ties between the Canadian and United States stoneware industries, it is difficult to determine the origin of manufacture except by maker's marks. Brush and slip-trailed decorations on Canadian stoneware are quite similar to those seen on U.S. stoneware. Clearly, decorators, as well as potters, must have moved northward. Perhaps the most distinctive decorations found on Canadian stoneware are the elaborate molded and applied patterns most often associated with the potteries of Brantford, Canada West.

20.0 Jar (color plate)
F.P. Goold & Company (active 1859-1867)
Brantford, Ontario, 1859-1867
Height 14½"

Cylindrical jar of salt-glazed stoneware with rounded lip and fat handles applied below the rim. The decoration, consisting of two birds standing on a banner, is delicately incised and filled with blue in the manner of U.S. stoneware decoration of several decades earlier. A zig-zag coggle and small star-shaped stamp were also used for embellishment. **(E)**

Royal Ontario Museum, Canadiana Department

20.1 Jar
Cornwall Pottery (active 1869-1907)
Cornwall, Ontario, c. 1880-1885
Height 11"

Cylindrical jar of salt-glazed stoneware with rounded rim, applied handles, and blue decoration of slip-trailed vine and grape cluster; impressed mark "CORN-WALL/POTTERY.C.W." below the rim. Operated by Flack and Van Arsdale, the Cornwall Pottery produced as much as $30,000 worth of ware per annum. **(D)**

D.B. Webster

20.2 Jar
George Lazier (active 1867-1887), operator of the Hart Pottery
Picton, Canada West, Ontario, 1867-1887
Height 11"

Salt-glazed stoneware jar with sloping shoulder, straight sides, thick rim, and handles applied to shoulder; decorated on side with blue slip-trailed flourish below handwritten "Pottoes [sic]" and "2"; impressed mark below rim "G.I.LAZIER/PICTON.C.W." **(C)**

20.3 Jug
Possibly Ballard Pottery (active c. 1858-1860)
St. Johns, Quebec, Canada
1858-1860
Height 14" (two-gallon capacity)

Salt-glazed stoneware jug with straight sides, sloping shoulder, and thick opening; decorated with large stylized flower (concentric circles with petals) and leaves in trailed blue slip; impressed with merchant's mark "WELLS & AUDY/MARCHAND EPICIERS/No. 54 56 RUE TS PIERRE/BASSE VILLE/Quebec." **(D)**

Royal Ontario Museum, Canadiana Department

20.4 Crock
George Lazier (active 1867-1887), the Hart Pottery
Picton, Canada West, Ontario, 1867-1887
Height 8⅝"

Salt-glazed stoneware crock with straight out-flaring sides, ogee rim, and applied handles in the form of spaniel heads; impressed mark below rim "3/G.I.LAZIER/PICTON.C.W."; simple blue sprig trailed beneath mark with vertical series of dashes. Lazier had his clays shipped from New Jersey. **(D)**

National Museum of Canada

20.5 Crock
William Hart & Company (1849-1855)
Picton, Prince Edward County, Ontario, c. 1850
Height 16"

Wheel-thrown stoneware crock with applied handles; salt-glazed and decorated with a flower and leaf (or bee) brushed on with cobalt blue; impressed mark "W^M HART & CO./PICTON, C.W." **(D)**

20.6 Spittoon
Medalta Potteries, Ltd.
    (1916-1958; 1966-present)
Medicine Hat, Alberta, c. 1920
Height 5¼"

Slip-cast stoneware spittoon with low relief decoration of scrolls; pale blue glaze overall; marked on the base "MEDALTA POTTERIES, LTD./MEDICINE HAT/ALBERTA". Medalta has had a very large business in stoneware containers and other forms for food and beverage service for many years. **(A)**

Royal Ontario Museum, Canadiana Department

21 | Stoneware: Modern Revivals

Utilitarian stoneware continues to be produced in a few large midwestern factories as well as in several small, traditional southern potteries where alkaline-glazed coarse stoneware is still made. In addition to these instances of a continuing tradition, there are several modern potteries making stoneware in early shapes with traditional decorations.

One of the earliest examples of this phenomenon is the Jugtown Pottery in Jugtown, North Carolina, founded about 1920 by Jacques and Juliana Busbee. When the Busbees, as vacationers in North Carolina, stumbled across the work of traditional craftsmen in the area, they set about creating a viable market for their wares. Though produced in Jugtown, their wares were marketed primarily through Juliana's tearoom in Greenwich Village, New York. The work at Jugtown has been oriented towards the revival of a craft, rather than mere reproduction. Although the Busbees are deceased, the pottery is still in operation.

Because stoneware production by traditional hand methods is a series of difficult and costly operations, there are few reproduction potteries. Two, in particular, are associated with museums. The Williamsburg Pottery in Virginia, while not directly operated by Colonial Williamsburg, sells most of its production of small stoneware articles (as well as slip-decorated redware in the English manner) to the retail outlet of Colonial Williamsburg. Generally, they work in traditional shapes with incised decoration filled with cobalt blue. Their salt and pepper shakers, however, are a modern adaptation of an eighteenth-century sugar caster. Jugs and jars are also produced in the pottery operated by the Connor Prairie Restoration near Indianapolis, Indiana. Here the forms and decorations are typical of midwestern stoneware of the mid-nineteenth century.

For a brief period in the 1940s the Stangl Pottery in Trenton, New Jersey, produced hand-thrown stoneware vessels with brushed blue decorations in addition to their regular lines of dinnerwares and bird figures. The Stangl company descended from the Fulper Pottery, which had been in the stoneware business in Flemington, New Jersey, since c. 1810. Although the shapes and decorations of the Stangl reproduction wares could not be confused with the early-American originals, the general effect resembles the traditional products.

21.0 Jug (color plate)
Jugtown Pottery (1915-1958; 1960-present)
Jugtown, North Carolina, Current production
Height 10"

Traditional forms of stoneware continue to be made in a number of potteries in the southern highlands. The drips on this salt-glazed stoneware jug are from the accumulated salt in the kiln and the alkaline glazes from nearby pots. Vernon Owen, the maker of this jug, descended from several generations of North Carolina potters. **(A)**

Jugtown Pottery

21.1 Mugs
Williamsburg Pottery
Williamsburg, Virginia, current productions
Heights 5¾", 4½", 3½", 5" (right to left)

Gray salt-glazed mugs at right with cobalt blue decoration, inspired

by fragments from the Williamsburg archaeological collection. The design of the yellow and brown mug at left dates back to the early settlement at Jamestown, Virginia. **(A)**

Colonial Williamsburg Foundation

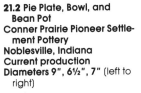

21.2 Pie Plate, Bowl, and Bean Pot
Conner Prairie Pioneer Settlement Pottery
Noblesville, Indiana
Current production
Diameters 9", 6½", 7" (left to right)

Wheel-thrown, salt-glazed stoneware, Albany slip interiors; stoneware in traditional forms is hand-made from local Clay County, Indiana clay. **(A)**

Conner Prairie Pioneer Settlement Pottery

21.3 Jar
Stangl Pottery (1929-1972, formerly Fulper Pottery)
Trenton, New Jersey, Dated 1941
Height 9"

Wheel-thrown ovoid jar of stoneware with applied handles, decorated on one side with blue painted flower and leaves and "1941" below; impressed mark near bottom "STANGL/STONEWARE". (See also 43: Mid-Atlantic Art Pottery and 50: Modern Tableware.) **(A)**

New Jersey State Museum

21.4 Pitcher
Brown's Pottery (1925-present)
Buncombe County, North Carolina, c. 1930
Height 12¾" (two-gallon capacity)

Wheel-thrown stoneware pitcher covered overall with Albany slip and Spanish whiting; impressed mark "BROWN/BROS". **(A)**

21.5 "Grotesque" Face Jug
Burlon B. Craig (1914-present)
Vale, Lincoln County, North Carolina, Recent
Height 10⅝" (one-gallon capacity)

Glossy, gray-green alkaline glaze on a stoneware jug, hand-modeled to resemble a face; impressed mark on bottom "B.B. CRAIG/VALE, N.C." **(A)**

22 | Yellow Ware: Rockingham

Yellow ware has a buff or yellowish color when fired, although it may be made of earthenware or stoneware. Because it is often difficult to determine the true nature of the body, the designation of yellow ware is sufficient as a collective reference. Much of this ware, whether earthenware or stoneware, was covered with a brown mottled glaze over a solid body or a yellow slip over a buff body. This is known as "Rockingham" because the ware was first produced in Swinton, England, on the property of the Marquis of Rockingham. "Bennington" is perhaps the word most commonly used for this ware in America because of the high quality of the work produced at the potteries in Bennington, Vermont, and because at least three books have been written about these potteries. Both terms, however, are misleading. In fact, brown mottled yellow ware was produced in many potteries from Massachusetts to Illinois and in Canada as well. Through widespread use by contemporary collectors the words "Rockingham" and "Bennington" have become generic terms.

Yellow ware with a brown mottled glaze which resembles tortoise shell, became extremely popular by the mid-nineteenth century in the United States and Canada in forms suitable for food and beverage preparation and service. Bowls, pitchers, and teapots are the most common forms encountered today. Sanitary wares like bedpans, cuspidors, and toilet sets (wash bowl, chamber pot, slop jar, etc.) were also made. These were all slip-cast in plaster molds and usually bear decoration in low relief beneath the glaze. Because English wares provided the prototypes, the decorations are generally English in inspiration.

Bowls were most often paneled; many survive with naturalistic or conventionalized scrolled leaf forms repeated around the sides. Pitchers are known with a variety of designs, from the simple chain and anchor (symbolic of hope), to the elaborate hunt scenes and still lifes popular at the time. These often have handles molded in the form of a hound. The Toby pitchers, molded in the form of a seated fat man drinking beer, were also fairly common.

Judging from the numbers that survive, the most desirable decoration to have on teapots was the Biblical vignette showing Rebeccah at the well. Many of these designs were so popular that no single pottery was solely responsible for all that are available on the market today. Desirability is determined by the quality (sharpness) of the molding and balance of the design. Figures, especially dogs and lions, were also made in Rockingham-glazed yellow ware, as well as bottles in the form of coachmen.

Marked examples of these wares are rare; however, unmarked pieces are often difficult to distinguish from English examples. Those manufacturers for which marked specimens might be found include the American Pottery Company, Jersey City, New Jersey; the Salamander Works of Woodbridge, New Jersey (marked with the address of the New York sales office); the Congress Pottery, South Amboy, New Jersey; the Bennett Pottery, Baltimore, Maryland; Harker, Taylor and Company, East Liverpool, Ohio; the Cap Rouge Pottery, Quebec; and the Brantford Stoneware Manufacturing Company, Ontario.

22.0 Teapot (color plate)
Edwin Bennett Pottery (active 1846-1938)
Baltimore, Maryland, c. 1850-1865
Height 9"

Yellow earthenware teapot molded with "Rebekah at the Well" pattern and covered with spotted brown glaze. Teapots with this pattern were made by many potteries in North America, although Edwin Bennett was the originator of the design. **(B)**

NMAH

22.1 Teapot
Southern Porcelain Company
(active 1856-1862)
Kaolin, South Carolina
1856-1862
Height 4½"

Yellow earthenware teapot molded with the "Rebekah at the Well" pattern; covered with green, red, and brown spotted glaze; molded mark "FIRE PROOF SPCo" on bottom. The company also made Parian, white wares, and telegraph insulators. **(C)**

NMAH

22.2 Teapot
Brantford Pottery (various owners 1849-1907)
Brantford, Ontario, c. 1880
Height 7½" (with lid)

Molded stoneware teapot with low relief pattern of a beaver on a log near the bottom with maple leaves above, rustic spout and handle; lid is in the form of a tree stump with a beaver reclining on top. **(C)**

Royal Ontario Museum, Canadiana Department

22.3 Pitcher
Harker, Taylor & Company (1847-c. 1850)
East Liverpool, Ohio, 1847-1850
Height 10"

Yellow earthenware pitcher molded with hunt scene in low relief around body; ogee shoulder, tall straight neck with ivy and high arched spout, standing hound handle; covered in drippy brown glaze. This company was one of the earliest in East Liverpool to make "Rockingham" wares. Impressed company mark is in a circle. **(C)**

NMAH

22.4 Pitcher
American Pottery Company (active 1833-1857)
Jersey City, New Jersey, c. 1840
Height 12"

Molded stoneware pitcher with low relief decorations of a deer chase around the body; grapes, vines, and leaves on the shoulder and neck; crouching hound handle. Mark impressed on bottom. Daniel Greatbach produced the first molds for hound-handled pitchers in America at the American Pottery Company. **(D)**

NMAH

22.5 Pitcher
**Salamander Works (active
1836-1842)
Woodbridge, New Jersey (with
salesrooms in New York City)
1836-1842
Height 11¼"**

Molded stoneware pitcher with
pear-shaped body and boat-
shaped neck and spout (with
strainer), ear-shaped scrolled
handle; low relief decorations of
acanthus leaves, grape vines,
satyr masks, and foliated double
scrolls; covered with glossy brown
glaze. According to an 1837 price
list, this pattern was made in five
sizes. **(D)**

NMAH

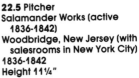

22.6 Pitcher
**Hanks & Fish, Swan Hill Pottery
South Amboy, New Jersey
c. 1849
Height 8⅝"**

Cylindrical pitcher of yellow earthenware with molded grape vine
pattern in low relief on textured
ground; handle in the form of a
vine; overall spotted brown glaze.
Marked with impressed swan
above "HANKS & FISH/SWAN HILL/
POTTERY/S AMBOY/NJ". **(C)**

NMAH

22.7 Pitcher
**William Bloor (1859-1862)
East Liverpool, Ohio, 1859-1862
Height 10⅛"**

Yellow earthenware pitcher molded with relief pattern of tulip clusters on the sides; ear-shaped handle; covered overall with a dark
brown glossy glaze. Along with associates, Mr. Bloor organized several potteries in East Liverpool, as
well as Trenton, New Jersey. **(C)**

NMAH

22.8 Pitcher
Cap Rouge Pottery (active c. 1860-1900)
Quebec, Quebec Province, c. 1880-1890
Height approximately 6"

Brown-glazed earthenware pitcher molded with relief motifs of cranes and foliage and a twisted vine handle. Incised mark on the bottom "Cap Rouge/Pottery". This pottery also produced the familiar "Rebekah at the Well" pattern. **(C)**

National Museum of Canada

22.9 Pitcher
Unidentified Maker
Probably New Jersey, c. 1880
Height 8½"

Yellow earthenware pitcher molded with horseback riders in low relief around the middle with leaves and branches at the top and bottom; branch handle; covered overall with a drippy, medium-brown glossy glaze. This pattern was made in several different sizes at various potteries in the Amboy-Matawan area of New Jersey. **(B)**

NMAH

22.10 Pitcher
Unidentified Maker
Probably Philadelphia,
   Pennsylvania, c. 1876
Height 10½"

Yellow earthenware pitcher molded with figure of George Washington standing next to partial stone wall and surrounded with leaves, branches, and flowers; ear-shaped handle; covered with dark brown glossy glaze. **(C)**

NMAH

22.11 Pitcher
Probably East Liverpool, Ohio, c. 1860
Height 10½"

Molded pitcher of yellow earthenware; octagonal shape with hound handle and design on sides of hanging game; an eagle on the spout; glazed overall in streaky brown and blue; unmarked. **(B)**

22.12 Spittoon
Boston Earthenware Mfg. Co.
  (active 1852-1858)
Boston, Massachusetts
1852-1858
Height 9½"

Yellow earthenware spittoon
molded in round scalloped shape
with twelve scallop shells in low relief around the top; paneled interi-
or; covered overall with a drippy,
brown-spotted glossy glaze. **(B)**

NMAH

22.13 Spittoon
Etruria Pottery (1844-c. 1876)
East Liverpool, Ohio, c. 1852
Diameter 7¼"

Molded spittoon of buff earthenware with a fluted pattern covered
with streaked and spattered, brown and blue glazes; molded mark on
bottom in a circle "ETRURIA WORKS/EAST LIVERPOOL, OHIO/1852." **(B)**

22.14 Figure
Unidentified maker
United States, 1850-1890
Height approximately 10"

Yellow earthenware molded figure of seated dog on scroll-deco-
rated rectangular plinth; covered
with glossy brown-spotted glaze.
The popularity of English Staffordshire mantel figures of spaniels
lead many American potteries to
produce imitations in a variety of
materials. **(C)**

NMAH

22.15 "Toby" Jug
Probably Ohio, c. 1870
Height 5⅛"

Molded pitcher of yellow earthenware in the shape of Toby Philpot
drinking from a mug while wearing a tricornered hat; splashed overall
with brown and covered in a clear glaze; unmarked. **(A)**

22.16 Butter Crock
London Crockery Mfg. Co. (1886-1888)
Pottersburg, London Township, Ontario, 1886-1888
Height 8"; Diameter 8½"

Molded crock of yellow earthenware in shallow ribbed design with applied handles; spotted brown Rockingham glaze; impressed mark on bottom "LONDON CROCKERY MFG. CO LONDON ONT." **(B-C)**

22.17 Jug
The Roycroft Shops (active
**   c. 1900-1938)**
East Aurora, New York, c. 1915
Height 5¾"

Small molded jug of a refined buff earthenware covered with glossy medium brown glaze. Impressed mark on bottom is the Roycroft orb surrounded by "THE ROYCROFT SHOPS/EAST AURORA, N.Y." Pottery was one of the many crafts executed by the Roycroft Shops, perhaps best known for their furniture, metal work, and book bindings. **(A)**

Private Collection

23 | Yellow Ware: Bennington

"Bennington" refers not to a specific company, but to a town in Vermont that is well-known for the pottery made there by several firms. These wares have been distinguished here from those of other companies which made brown-glazed yellow ware because so much more is known about the Bennington potteries. The generic use of the term "Bennington" to refer to all brown-glazed yellow ware is misleading because so many of the patterns made at other factories were not produced in Bennington. For example, "Rebekah-at-the-Well" teapots, which were so common, were never a product of the potteries of Bennington.

The several potteries which operated in Bennington were owned by various members of the Norton and Fenton families. Those which made tortoise-glazed pottery were Norton and Fenton (1845-47); Lyman, Fenton and Company (1849-52, mark used sporadically until 1858) and its successor, the United States Pottery Company (1852-58).

A wide variety of forms were produced in these factories, including pitchers, mugs, bedpans and toilet wares, Toby mugs, "coachman" bottles, figures of lions and poodles, cow creamers, doorknobs, vases, candlesticks, baking dishes, and bowls. Wares may be marked, although many fine pieces were left unmarked. Because these firms made such a variety of forms and because so many other North American factories were also producing these wares, the reader is referred to Richard Carter Barret's **Bennington Pottery and Porcelain** (see bibliography) as the best guide to determining if specific examples were made in the potteries of Bennington.

In 1849 Christopher Webber Fenton acquired a patent for applying color to yellow ware. Various metallic glaze colorants (for brown, blue, yellow, and green) were powdered onto the biscuit (or once-fired) ware, leaving some of the yellow body beneath to show. When fired a second time these oxides often mingled and flowed together producing beautiful, if largely accidental, effects. The use of powdered metallic oxides also produced brilliant coloring because the colors were not weakened by mixture with a clear glaze before application. The use of metallic oxides to produce a multicolored tortoise shell glaze was not new. Even the application of these oxides in powdered form had been used previously on various types of pottery. Fenton's product, however, is quite distinctive. The ware was called "flint enamel" to denote the brilliantly shiny glaze. While examples often bear the large oval mark which refers to the patent date of 1849 below the Lyman, Fenton & Co. name, there are a number of marked pieces known which do not have the flint enamel glaze. The reason for this is simply that workmen at the pottery were careless.

Many collectors consider the actual Bennington-made products to be more desirable than examples of brown-glazed yellow wares from other factories. This prejudice is probably related to the fact that much less has been written about the fine wares made by lesser-known companies.

23.0 Four Flasks (color plate)
United States Pottery Company (1847-1858)
Bennington, Vermont, 1849-1858
Heights 8" and 11"

Four examples of the colorful flint enamel glaze on yellow earthenware for which C.W. Fenton was issued a patent in 1849. **Battle of Bennington, Life of Kossuth,** and **Hermit's Delight** were among the popular titles chosen for these disguised flasks. **(C, each)**

Bennington Museum

23.1 Pitcher
United States Pottery Company (1847-1858)
Bennington, Vermont, 1849-1858
Height 9½"

Molded pitcher of yellow earthenware in "Swirled Alternate Rib" pattern with scrolled ear-shaped handle and high arching spout; covered overall in a glossy brown-spotted glaze. R. C. Barret identified this as a rare pattern. **(C-D)**

NMAH

23.2 Book Flasks
United States Pottery Company (1847-1858)
Bennington, Vermont, 1849-1858
Heights 10½", 6⅛", 8⅛" (left to right)

Flasks in the shape of books molded from yellow earthenware and covered with "Rockingham" and flint enamel glazes. Some potteries in New Jersey and Ohio also produced book flasks imitating the Bennington product. The Bennington examples, however, show greater attention to detail and fine workmanship. **(C-D, each)**

NMAH

23.3 Cream Pitcher
**Attributed to the United States
  Pottery Company (1847-1858)**
Bennington, Vermont, 1849-1858
Height 5¾"

Yellow earthenware creamer molded in the form of a cow with raised tail, standing on an oval plinth and covered with a mottled light brown glaze. Cow creamers were made at many potteries. According to R. C. Barret, the Bennington-made examples have an open mouth, open eyes, crescent-shaped nostrils, and distinct rib and neck folds. **(C)**

NMAH

23.4 Pitcher
Lyman, Fenton & Company (1849-1852)
Bennington, Vermont, c. 1850
Height 7½"

Octagonal pitcher of yellow ware in "tulip and heart" pattern and covered with splashed brown, blue, and yellow flint enamel glaze overall; impressed mark on bottom "Fenton's ENAMEL/PATENTED 1849/BENNINGTON, VT." **(C)**

23.5 Figures of Poodles
United States Pottery Company (1847-1858)
Bennington, Vermont, 1849-1858
Height 9¼"

Yellow earthenware figures molded in the shape of poodles holding baskets of flowers in their mouths. The fur was made by forcing clay through coarse cloth. The figures are covered overall by a glossy brown-streaked glaze. Fenton produced these poodles as mantel ornaments in plain yellow, Parian, and granite ware as well. **(E, pair)**

NMAH

23.6 "Coachman" Bottle
United States Pottery Company (1847-1858)
Bennington, Vermont, 1849-1858
Height 10⅛"

Bottle made of yellow earthen-

ware molded in the form of a man
with hat and cloak; covered overall with a glossy brown-spotted
glaze. The original design of these
bottles is thought to be the work of
the modeler, Daniel Greatbach,
who had previously worked for the
American Pottery Company in
Jersey City, N.J. **(C)**

NMAH

24 | Yellow Ware: Plain and Colored Glazes

In addition to the tortoise shell effects already described, yellow ware
was made with plain and colored glazes. These were molded wares
manufactured for use in food preparation and beverage service, but
not usually for use as dinnerware. Bowls, pie plates, pitchers, mugs,
and food molds were the most common forms.

Often the yellow earthenware body was left undecorated to show
through the clear glaze. These wares could be further decorated with
plain bands of white, blue, or black slip or with wider bands into which
dendritic (tree-like) ornaments were introduced. Forms which were
left plain or decorated with bands include bowls, pitchers, and mugs
patterned directly after English banded or mocha wares. Because
the same methods were used in both places it is very difficult to distinguish English from American examples except in the rare instances
where marks are present.

In some cases a yellowish clay slip was applied over a buff-colored
stoneware which might also be dipped at the top or bottom in dark
brown slip. D. & J. Henderson of Jersey City, New Jersey (1829-33), produced some fine pitchers of this type molded with low relief figures or
in the popular "Toby" form. The technique was in use in England by
the early eighteenth century, while comparatively few were made in
America. Caution should be used, therefore, in assigning an American origin to unmarked examples.

Brilliant multicolored glazes on rather coarse, buff-colored earthenware came into fashion about 1870 in American and England. The
ware is referred to as "majolica" after the tin-glazed wares made in
Italy from the sixteenth century onward. The nineteenth-century American and English products, however, bear little resemblance to the
Italian originals. American majolica was molded with low relief patterns of shells, seaweed, leaves, or with complex designs reminiscent
of the Orient. Pink, green, turquoise, and light blue over the yellow
body were the predominant colors suspended in a clear, shiny glaze.
The rather porous glaze and body of this ware stain easily. Unmarked

examples are difficult to distinguish from pieces made in England.

The best-known manufacturer of American majolica is perhaps the Griffen, Smith and Hill Company of Phoenixville, Chester County, Pennsylvania, which produced "Etruscan Majolica" from 1879 until about 1890. Tablewares and ornamental objects were made in patterns incorporating shells, seaweed, coral, and dolphin figures. Some forms were adapted from Irish Belleek porcelain.

24.0 Pitcher and Sugar Bowl (color plate)
Pitcher: American Pottery Company, Jersey City, N.J., (1833-1857)
Sugar Bowl: Griffen, Smith & Hill, Phoenixville, Pennsylvania
(1879-1890)
Pitcher: c. 1840, Sugar Bowl: 1879-1890
Height, pitcher 8¾"; height, sugar bowl 4¾"

Both examples are of molded yellow earthenware, the pitcher covered with clear glaze, the sugar bowl in the shape of a cauliflower with green and pink glazes. These wares with coarse body and glaze chip and discolor easily. (See 22.4 for same A.P.C. mold in brown-glazed stoneware.) **(D, pitcher; B, sugar bowl)**

New Jersey State Museum

24.1 Dish
Abraham Cadmus, Congress
**   Pottery (active 1849-1854)**
South Amboy, New Jersey
c. 1850
Diameter 9⅝"

Wheel-thrown dish of yellow earthenware with flat bottom and straight out-flaring sides. Mark impressed on bottom "`-ADMUS, CONGRESS POTTERY/SOUTH AMBOY/NJ". An enormous quantity of yellow ware forms for food preparation and beverage service were made by many North American potteries. Few examples, however, are marked. **(B; A if unmarked)**

New Jersey State Museum

24.2 Bowl
Cap Rouge Pottery (active
**   c. 1860-1900)**
Quebec, Quebec Province
c. 1870-1890
Diameter 9⅜"

Utility bowl of buff earthenware
with bands of white, brown, and
blue slip and clear glaze overall.
Yellow ware bowls, mugs, and
pitchers were made in large
quantities in North American potteries and in England as well.
Marked examples are extremely
rare. **(B; A, unmarked)**

Royal Ontario Museum, Canadiana Department

24.3 Mixing Bowl
Probably Ohio, c. 1900
Height 6"; Diameter 9½"

Molded round bowl of yellow earthenware with shallow-relief scroll
decoration covered overall with sponged brown and green glazes
popularly known as "gypsy spatter." **(A)**

24.4 Teapot
Attributed to A. Hall & Sons
(active c. 1865-?)
Perth Amboy, New Jersey
Late 19th century
Height 8¾" (with cover)

Yellow earthenware teapot molded in an oval shape with rounded
foot; vertical fluting on neck,
cover, and finial; applied letters
on one side of body "R. F. WHITE/
PERTH AMBOY./N.J.", for whom the
pot was made. Spotted brown,
green, and blue glaze. **(D)**

New Jersey State Museum

24.5 Food Mold
Ira W. Cory Pottery (c. 1868-1869)
Trenton, New Jersey, c. 1868-1869
Length 8½"

Oval food mold of yellow ware with design of pineapple and vines with
fruit, leaf border; clear glaze overall; impressed mark "I.W.CORY". **(A)**

24.6 Teapot
**Griffen, Smith & Hill (active
1879-1890)
Phoenixville, Pennsylvania
1879-1890
Height 5¾"**

Molded hexagonal teapot of yellow earthenware with bird and grass design on the two long sides; bamboo handle; layered, scalloped spout; colored majolica glazes. This company produced large quantities of ware for tea services. **(B)**

NMAH

24.7 Crock
**Tara Pottery, James McCluskie (1867-1884)
Tara, Lake Simcoe Region, Ontario, c. 1880
Height 15¼"**

Wheel-thrown crock of yellow earthenware with clear lead glaze overall; impressed mark at shoulder "TARA POTTERY." **(B)**

24.8 Piggy Bank
**United States, probably Ohio
1850-1900
Length 5¾"**

Molded pig of cream-colored earthenware with randomly sponged blue and pink decoration and clear lead glaze overall. Novelty banks such as this one were made in many potteries throughout the eastern and midwestern United States. **(B)**

Private Collection

24.9 Pitcher
**Ohio, c. 1900
Height 8"**

Molded cylindrical pitcher of buff earthenware, glazed overall with white "Bristol" slip and decorated on the outside with coarsely sponged cobalt blue; unmarked. **(B)**

25 | White Ware: Plain Molded

White ware is loosely defined as any white earthenware or semi-porcelain which is opaque. This includes wares made to imitate porcelain but lacking the translucency of the finer ware because of the type of clays used or the thickness of the piece.

The production of cream-colored wares in imitation of the varieties of English pieces available during the late eighteenth and early nineteenth centuries was doubtless practiced in America to an extent far greater than is now understood. It is known from archaeological excavations, for example, that such wares were made by Rudolph Christ in the Moravian pottery at Salem, North Carolina, during this period. Newspaper evidence also points to the manufacture of these wares in Philadelphia and Boston as well. Definitely attributable examples of such American-made wares, however, are so difficult to distinguish from their English counterparts that they have not been included in this volume.

By the mid-nineteenth century American refined earthenwares became more recognizable, partly because of the decorations, but primarily because manufacturers often marked their wares.

Ironstone, stone china, or white granite, as it is variously known, is a highly refined, opaque earthenware distinguished by a bluish tinge and often a fine crackle in the glaze. Although it may be decorated, ironstone shows to best advantage in the plain white wares molded in low relief patterns popular during the second half of the nineteenth century for tablewares, tea wares, kitchen crockery, and toilet wares. Large tureens and coffeepots are particularly impressive in plain white ironstone. Common patterns included wheat, berries, and various leaf forms in addition to the undecorated wares, and specialty pieces such as bread plates with the proverbial invocation to "Give Us This Day Our Daily Bread."

Ironstone was an inexpensive, sturdy ware. Because it is basically an earthenware, however, ironstone discolors when subjected to heat or prolonged contact with moisture or foodstuffs. It is not unusual to find ironstone chipped, cracked, or stained simply because it was used daily and was never intended to be kept in the cupboard for the most important dining occasions in the way fine china was protected.

Ironstone was an English invention, but, by the 1870s, it was produced in great quantities in North America as well. In East Liverpool, Ohio, Laughlin Brothers (1879-1897, thereafter Homer Laughlin China Company), Burgess and Company (?-1893), Globe Pottery Company (established 1881), and Great Western Pottery Works (established 1868), among many others, manufactured white granite wares for a number of years. About 1865, Taylor and Speeler, the Glasgow Pottery of John Moses, and the Etruria Pottery of Ott and Brewer began the long tradition of ironstone manufacture in Trenton, New Jersey; soon to be followed by the Greenwood Pottery Company (beginning in 1868), the International Pottery Company (established 1878, later Burgess & Campbell), the Willets Manufacturing Company (established 1879), Dale and Davis (beginning in 1880), and many others.

George Whitefield Farrar is credited with being the first manufacturer of white ware in Canada when he established the St. Johns Stone

Chinaware Company in 1873 in Quebec. In addition to the standard ironstone wares, the company also made a small amount of ironstone with the body tinted blue throughout and small white decorations sprigged on in imitation of Wedgwood's jasper ware. Following fires and serious financial problems, the St. Johns Stone Chinaware Company closed by 1899. The manufacture of ironstone was not successfully attempted again in Canada until 1934 when Sovereign Potteries Ltd., Hamilton, Ontario, was organized.

The enthusiast wishing to acquire examples of American-made ironstone should concentrate on marked pieces because English and American patterns are generally quite similar. It is important, also, that marks not be looked at casually. Many American firms identified their wares with emblems that were close in appearance to the British coat of arms, the variations evident only in the letters or names that surround the emblem.

25.0 Ellsworth Pitcher (color plate)
Millington, Astbury and Poulson (1859-1870)
Trenton, New Jersey, 1861
Height 8½"

Molded ironstone pitcher with low relief decoration which illustrates the shooting of Col. E.E. Ellsworth at Alexandria, Virginia, at the beginning of the Civil War. Modeled by Josiah Jones, examples are known with brilliant blue and red coloring, as well as white, and in ironstone bodies of varying quality. **(D)**

NMAH

25.1 Pitcher
Stone Chinaware Company
 (active 1874-1899)
St. Johns, Quebec, c. 1885
Height 11¾"

Ribbed, pear-shaped pitcher of molded ironstone with loop handle; relief decorations of wheat around handle terminals with acanthus leaf below the spout. Black printed mark on bottom of the British arms with "STONE CHINAWARE CO." above and "ST. JOHNS, P.Q." below. **(B)**

The Montreal Museum of Fine Arts

25.2 Pitcher
Greenwood Pottery Company
(1868-1933)
Trenton, New Jersey, c. 1875
Height 9¼"

Heavy ironstone pitcher molded
with spout in the shape of a
walrus's head. On one side is a
scene showing King Gambrinus,
reputed originator of lager beer,
offering a large glass of the foam-
ing Teutonic beverage to Uncle
Sam. On the reverse is a scene
from a poem by Bret Harte (1870)
about a Chinese cardsharp. **(D)**

New Jersey State Museum

25.3 Pitcher
Cook Pottery Company (active 1894-1931)
Trenton, New Jersey, c. 1900
Height 6¾"

Bread Tray
Bloor, Ott and Brewer (active 1865-1871)
Trenton, New Jersey, 1865-1871
Length 12"

Both examples were manufactured in Trenton and molded from plain
white ironstone. Both manufacturers marked these wares with the
British arms and individual company initials on the bottom. Trenton was
an important center of ironstone production during the nineteenth
century. **(A, pitcher; B, tray)**

New Jersey State Museum

25.4 Bread Tray
Stone Chinaware Company (active 1874-1899)
St. Johns, Quebec, c. 1885
Length 13¼"

Oval bread tray of lightly tinted blue ironstone molded with a sheaf of wheat in the center, wheat and scroll pattern at each end, and the motto "WASTE NOT/WANT NOT" raised on the border. The initials and flower sprig (made to special order) were formed by applying white ironstone. **(B)**

25.5 Plate
Stone Chinaware Company
(active 1874-1899)
St. Johns, Quebec, 1880-1890
Diameter 8½"

Molded ironstone plate of medium blue tinted body with monogram and two flower sprigs of applied white ironstone. The plate is part of a dinner service. Production of "blue ware" was a peculiarity of the St. Johns Stone Chinaware Company. **(A)**

The Montreal Museum of Fine Arts

25.6 Sugar Bowl
New England Pottery Company (1875-c. 1910)
East Boston, Massachusetts, c. 1888
Height 4¼"

Molded sugar bowl of semi-porcelain; tinted blue and having a globular shape with two handles and a cover; mark printed in black on bottom reads "RIETI" below arm and dagger. **(A)**

25.7 Child's Tea Set
Ott and Brewer's Etruria Pottery (1871-1892)
Trenton, New Jersey, 1880-1890
Height, teapot 5½"

Part of a charming child's ironstone tea set consisting of teapot, sugar bowl, cream pitcher, six plates, and six cups and saucers. Complete sets are rare. The mark suggests English origin, except for the "O & B" cipher in the middle. **(B, set)**

New Jersey State Museum

25.8 Citrus Juicer
Thomas Maddock's Sons (1902-1929)
Trenton, New Jersey, 1900-1910
Height overall 4½"; Width 4¾"

Octagonal juicer of molded ironstone in two parts, the top section with scalloped edge. Mark includes notation "MADE OF/DUROCK/ACID PROOF." Durock was the trade name for a sturdy, high-fired material which this company used primarily for sanitary equipment. **(A)**

New Jersey State Museum

25.9 Brush Holder
Thomas Maddock's Sons (1902-1929)
Trenton, New Jersey, 1900-1910
Height 5⅝"; Length 10⅝"

Open box of molded ironstone with holes on the back for mounting on a wall. The size and plainness of this box suggest that it was meant to hold a utility brush. There is a drain hole in the bottom and a large printed black mark of an anchor surrounded by a belt with the company name. **(A)**

New Jersey State Museum

25.10 Chamber Pot
Mayer Pottery Manufacturers (1881-?)
Beaver Falls, Pennsylvania
c. 1885
Height 5⅝"; Length overall 10¼"

Chamber pot of heavy molded ironstone with leafy square handle. Mark printed on bottom shows British arms with an "M" in the middle, the words "IRONSTONE CHINA" above, and "MAYER POTTERY M'F'S CO" below. The pot probably had a lid originally. **(A)**

New Jersey State Museum

26 | White Ware: Printed Tablewares

Finer earthenwares were in production by 1840 at the American Pottery Manufacturing Company in Jersey City, New Jersey, for it was about this time that the famous Harrison pitcher was made for the Presidential campaign. The pitcher is decorated with transfer prints of a log cabin, American eagle, and portrait of William Henry Harrison. The blue transfer-printed "Canova" pattern taken from a design by John Ridgway of Hanley, England, was also made by this Jersey City firm about the same time.

Transfer printing is a decorative technique which depends on a copperplate engraving for multiple copy productions. The engraved copperplate is "inked" with the proper color, after which a print is pulled from the plate on tissue. The tissue is carefully rubbed, ink side down, into the biscuit-fired surface, thereby transferring the print from copperplate to pottery. The technique was developed in England during the 1750s but was not used in America until the nineteenth century. Although some transfer printing of earthenware was probably done prior to the Harrison pitcher and Canova plate mentioned above, the use of the process before 1840 is not well documented at this time. By the second half of the nineteenth century, however, transfer printing was quite common in America as a cheap, but effective, method of achieving detailed decorations. With this mechanical process skilled decorators were not needed for the more exacting hand-executed decoration. Semiskilled workers could easily produce the elaborate printed designs. Hand coloring of transfer-printed designs was also accomplished by semiskilled workers. The combination of printing and painting was used to a great extent after 1880 to enhance tablewares.

A larger variety of forms than we commonly use today constituted the typical table setting during the nineteenth century. In addition to the soup, dinner, salad, bread plates (before 1890 used for baked potatoes rather than bread), and dessert plates, the Victorian table setting included a small round plate to hold an individual serving of butter, as well as a larger crescent-shaped dish (called a "crescent" in the past, but referred to as a "bone" dish today) used for discarded bones or for separating certain cold sauces and salads from the hot foods on the dinner plate. Towards the end of the nineteenth century the most complete table services provided several small plates (for appetizers, finger bowls, etc.), a service or "waiting" plate to elevate the appetizer and soup plates from the table, and a cup and plate **en suite** for sherbet (to clear the palate after the main course).

Not everyone, of course, dined with this much crockery. Table services could be purchased complete or, as was more commonly the case, only in part—the basic pieces first, the more frivolous pieces later as funds permitted. Recent research into merchants' account books suggests that consumers, particularly those in rural areas, rarely purchased a complete set. For this reason the survival of a complete dinner service from the nineteenth century is extremely rare.

Many companies, particularly in East Liverpool, Ohio, and Trenton, New Jersey, produced tablewares with printed decorations during the second half of the nineteenth century. The Dresden Pottery Company (1875-1892), Laughlin Brothers (1877-97, survives as Homer Laughlin China Co.), and the Knowles, Taylor & Knowles Company (1870-1934) are among the many East Liverpool manufacturers who made popular dinner wares. Trenton manufacturers included those companies mentioned under the previous category, as well as the Burroughs & Mountford Company (established 1879), Mercer Pottery Company (organized in 1868), Cook and Hancock's Crescent Pottery (established 1881), and the American China Company (using a chromolithographic process) in addition to others.

26.0 Plate (color plate)
American Pottery Company (1833-1857)
Jersey City, New Jersey, c. 1840
Diameter 9"

Molded plate of white earthenware with blue transfer print of pseudo-classical scene in the center and four small scenes on the border alternating with bunches of flowers. Mark printed in blue under the glaze in an oval "AMERICAN POTTY/MANUFACTURING Cº./JERSEY CITY"; above is an urn with "Canova/Stone ware" printed on base. **(B)**

New Jersey State Museum

26.1 Plate
C.H. Cook & W.S. Hancock, The Crescent Pottery Company (active 1881-1892, afterwards one of Trenton Potteries)
Trenton, New Jersey, c. 1890
Diameter 10⅛"

Rather heavy ironstone plate molded with four panels on the rim; brown transfer-print decoration of roses, stems, and leaves hand-colored with pink, yellow, and brown. Black printed mark on back with lion in round frame,

26.2 Pitcher
Anchor Pottery (1894-1926)
Trenton, New Jersey, c. 1898
Height 8"

Molded ironstone pitcher with arching spout and ear-shaped handle; transfer decorated on one side with a brown eagle and flags with hand-painted red stripes, and on the other side with an eagle alone. Possibly made in patriotic commemoration of the Spanish-American War. **(A)**

New Jersey State Museum

"SEMI-GRANITE" above and
"COOK & HANCOCK" below. **(A)**

New Jersey State Museum

26.3 Covered Pitcher
Ott and Brewer's Etruria Pottery
(1871-1892)
Trenton, New Jersey, c. 1880
Height 9"

Molded ironstone pitcher decorated with underglaze blue printed tulips and sponged gold. Rising sun mark on bottom. **(A)**

New Jersey State Museum

26.4 Covered Pitcher
Burroughs & Mountford Company
(1879-1882)
Trenton, New Jersey, 1879-1882
Height 9"

Molded ironstone pitcher covered with a cream-colored matte glaze intended to simulate bisque porcelain; transfer decorated with pink wisteria. The bamboo-like handles are striped with gold. Marked in gold on bottom "B. & M." below a crown. **(A)**

New Jersey State Museum

26.5 Footed Compote
Maddock Pottery Company
(1893-c. 1923)
Trenton, New Jersey, 1893-1923
Height 9¹¹/₁₆"; Diameter 7⁹/₁₆"

Compote molded of heavy semi-porcelain (hotel ware) and decorated with underglaze blue printed borders in a Renaissance-Revival pattern. Marked on bottom "M/ CHINA/L" for Maddock's pottery works in the Lamberton section of Trenton. **(A)**

New Jersey State Museum

26.6 Mug
Goodwin Pottery Company
(1893-1905)
East Liverpool, Ohio, c. 1900
Height 4¾"

Molded semi-porcelain mug decorated with a transfer-print scene
of a monk smelling a carnation in
white reserve on dark brown shaded ground. Part of a set including
a tankard pitcher and six mugs.
The mark in red on bottom shows a
sea dragon with "USONA" above
and "Goodwin" below. **(A)**

Courtesy of A. Richard Coleman

27 | White Ware: Printed Toilet Wares

Frequent personal washing was not commonplace prior to the mid-
nineteenth century. From that time, however, until the development
and general use of indoor plumbing, matched crockery toilet sets
displayed and used on washstands were a necessity for every bed-
room. The technique of transfer printing, as described previously, was
also applied to mundane toilet crockery made of ironstone or semi-
porcelain.

The standard toilet set of the late nineteenth century included a
covered chamber pot, covered slop jar, bowl and pitcher, covered
soap dish mug, toothbrush holder (either vase form or covered dish),
and covered sponge holder. Occasionally a small pitcher for water
was also added. These separate pieces were molded and decorated to match. In addition to white, colored or gilt bands offered the
plainest decoration. Simple and complex floral arrangements
printed on each piece were also extremely popular.

Upper class urban homes might be outfitted with porcelain sets,
while middle-class and rural homes owned any of the numerous kinds
of ironstone or semi-porcelain sets available on the market. The thinness of the ceramic body and delicacy of the transfer-printed decoration were the measures of quality. In general, the companies that
manufactured tablewares also made toilet wares because the same
technology was required for the production of both (see previous
white ware categories).

As a result of the development of indoor plumbing during the late
nineteenth century and the gradual incorporation of these conveni-
ences into domestic and public buildings, some companies specialized exclusively in sanitary fixtures. Although bathtubs, sinks, and
toilets are beyond the scope of this volume, it should be remembered
that these fixtures are still made of a highly refined white ceramic
body. Some of the most important of these specialty companies were

in Trenton, New Jersey, including John Maddock & Sons (established 1894), Standard Sanitary Manufacturing Company (1901-1943, now American Standard Inc.), and the Trenton Potteries Company (organized in 1892 by consolidation of five companies). Maddock was the son of Thomas Maddock, whose Trenton firm produced tablewares and sanitary earthenware for many years prior to the formation of John's company.

27.0 Bowl and Pitcher (color plate)
The Glasgow Pottery of John Moses & Company (active 1863-1895; with sons 1895-1905)
Trenton, New Jersey, c. 1880
Height, pitcher 12⅝"; Diameter, bowl 15"

Molded ironstone pitcher and bowl with brown transfer-printed decoration of roses and rose buds detached around surface and colored with red, pink, and several shades of green. Mark printed in black of British arms with "GPCo" in place of quarterings and "IRONSTONE CHINA/J.M.&Co." beneath. **(B)**

New Jersey State Museum

27.1 Shaving Mug
Ott & Brewer's Etruria Pottery (1871-1892)
Trenton, New Jersey, 1871-1892
Height 3¼"

Cylindrical ironstone mug with black printed design of two Roman soldiers on both sides and gold band at rim. Mark printed over the glaze in black shows lion and unicorn arms with "O & B" in center, "ETRURIA" above, and "STONE CHINA" below. Ott & Brewer made fine porcelain, but useful white wares were their staple. **(A)**

New Jersey State Museum

27.2 Toothbrush Holder
Maddock Pottery Company (1893-c.1923)
Trenton, New Jersey, c. 1894
Height 5⅛"

Cylindrical toothbrush holder of molded ironstone decorated with transfer print of red roses. Despite the humble material, the mark refers to the ware as "ROYAL PORCELAIN." Made in Maddock's Lamberton works. Part of a larger toilet set. **(A)**

New Jersey State Museum

27.3 Chamber Pot
Ott & Brewer's Etruria Pottery
(1871-1892)
Trenton, New Jersey, c. 1890
Height, including cover, 8½"

Molded ironstone chamber pot decorated with brown transfer-printed tulips, colored pink in reserves on a molded scallop-diaper ground. Printed Ott & Brewer sunrise mark on bottom. **(A)**

New Jersey State Museum

28 | White Ware: Printed Commercial and Commemorative

In addition to dinnerwares decoratively printed with patterns and intended for domestic use, many firms also made commercial ironstone and semi-porcelain tablewares which also were embellished with patterns. Because of the transferable print and chromolithographic processes, manufacturers could offer pieces with patterns to order in large or small quantities. Souvenir items, china for the dining rooms of hotels, railroads, and steamships, and even wares made as advertising giveaways, could all be reproduced many times using molds for the shapes and various print techniques for the decoration. Items in this category offer a wide range of possibilities for the collector.

Dinner services for use by hotels, railroads, and steamships are of necessity made of sturdy semi-porcelain. The amount of abuse to which these wares are subjected requires the china to be heavy and rather thick with a nonporous glaze and vitrified body. Commercial white ware such as this does not chip, crack, or stain easily. Most that is available to collectors today was made during this century, primarily by several New Jersey and Ohio companies that specialized in the institutional market. The Scammell China Company of Trenton, New Jersey, is a good example of one of these firms.

Some of the twenty buildings staffed by the 325 employees of the Scammell China Company in 1953 may have been part of the complex used earlier by the Trenton China Company, which started in 1859. The firm produced a fine grade of vitrified china until 1893 when the property was purchased by Thomas Maddock & Sons, manufacturers of dinnerwares and sanitary earthenwares. In 1923 the Scammell Brothers bought the plant and produced a wide range of hotel and restaurant china of very high quality, as well as a line of domestic dinnerware, until 1953.

Patterns produced by institutional china firms are of two general types: logos or special designs of a company which are made to order, or stock patterns purchased by many institutions. The first category includes items such as the Greenwood Pottery plate for Maxim's restaurant. Examples of the latter category may be seen in diners and restaurants all over the country. Common borders on the wares made for general use include the Greek key, conventional leaf patterns, or plain bands. Undecorated services are also available. The Syracuse (New York) China Corporation, Homer Laughlin (East Liverpool, Ohio), and the Buffalo (New York) China Company are among the largest manufacturers of these wares today. Quality is determined by thinness of the body.

Souvenir items also come under this commercial category. These include plates and other forms made to commemorate special events (such as the Scammell plate for the 1939 New York World's Fair), as a memento of a place visited, such as Niagara Falls, or to celebrate a particular institution, such as an historic house or church.

Advertising and calendar plates were especially popular during the late nineteenth and early twentieth centuries. Decorations on these plates were of several varieties: a large calendar in the center with company name above or below and a border of leaves, flowers, or scrolls; an identifying logo or picture in the center with calendar and/or firm name and border; or a picture alone with firm name and border. Although many of these were produced in Europe—or the European-made blanks were embellished by American decorating firms—a large number were manufactured by American companies. The plate pictured in 28.5 is an excellent example made by the Willets Manufacturing Company of Trenton.

28.0 Three Pitchers (color plate)
Left to right:
Charles Coxon & Co., Trenton, N.J. (1863-1884), Height 5½"
Ott & Brewer, Trenton, N.J. (1871-1892), Height 7⅞"
I. Davis, Trenton, N.J. (1875-1880), Height 7⅜"

All three of these ironstone pitchers were made to commemorate the Centennial Exposition in Philadelphia in 1876. The Coxon example depicts the Art Gallery; Ott & Brewer's shows the Art Gallery and Horticultural Hall with advertising for the Lafayette Restaurant; the Davis pitcher shows Horticultural Hall also. Engraved and lithographic printing processes made timely ceramic decoration inexpensive and popular. **(B, each)**

New Jersey State Museum

28.1 Tankard Pitcher
Thomas Maddock's Sons
   Company (1902-1929)
Trenton, New Jersey, Dated 1911
Height 12⁵⁄₁₆"

Pitcher molded of white ironstone
with commemorative inscription
printed in blue for a meeting of the
United Commercial Travelers of
America, New Jersey-Delaware
Grand Council, in Trenton, June
9-10, 1911. Note that the logo includes a small suitcase with the initials "U.C.T." The seal of the city of
Trenton is on the reverse. **(A)**

New Jersey State Museum

28.2 Cup and Saucer
The Glasgow Pottery of John
   Moses & Co. (active 1863-1895;
   with sons 1895-1905)
Trenton, New Jersey, c. 1876
Height, cup 2"; Diameter,
   saucer 5¼"

Hemispherical cup and round
saucer of ironstone; painted in
black on cup is "M. Washington"
and "1776" while saucer has printed legend "1776-1876/*First* Centennial * of * American * Indepen-
dence * Cincinnati". Made for
Women's Centennial Committee
in Cincinnati to raise money. Printed mark on bottom "GLASGOW
POTTERY CO./TRENTON, N.J." **(B)**

New Jersey State Museum

28.3 Plate
Greenwood Pottery Company
   (c. 1868-1933)
Trenton, New Jersey, c. 1910-1915
Diameter 8⅞"

Jigger-molded round plate of
semi-porcelain with transfer litho-
graph in brown, beige, and blue
with scrolled cartouche and
"Maxim's" in center, flanked by
two satyrs and band of geometric
shapes around rim. Impressed
mark on bottom "GREENWOOD
CHINA/TRENTON, N.J./REG: US.PAT.
OFF." **(A)**

New Jersey State Museum

28.4 Souvenir Plate
Scammell China Company
(1923-1953)
Trenton, New Jersey, 1939, for the
New York World's Fair
Diameter 11⅛"

Jigger-molded semi-porcelain plate, transfer printed in medium blue with a fanciful scene in the center of George Washington looking from a balcony at the Trilon and Perisphere of the Fair; eight scenes of the Fair around the border. Marked on reverse as official souvenir. **(A)**

New Jersey State Museum

28.5 Advertising Plate
Willets Manufacturing Company
(1879-1909)
Trenton, New Jersey, c. 1890
Diameter 8⁷⁄₁₆"

Round jigger-molded plate with scalloped rim; black transfer print in the center of half-figure of a man leaning his elbow on the scrolled arm of a couch; printed in gold beneath "COMPLIMENTS OF/ BRAND'S CREDIT PALACE/COM-PLETE OUTFITTERS & HOUSEFUR-NISHERS" with Trenton address. Mark on bottom printed in red octagon with "SEMI/W.M.Cº/PORCE-LAIN". **(A)**

New Jersey State Museum

28.6 Plate
Buffalo Pottery Company (active
1901-1956; survives today as
Buffalo China)
Buffalo, New York, Dated 1911
Diameter 4½"

Small white earthenware plate, jigger-molded and transfer-printed in dark green with a view of the Wanamaker store in Phila-delphia. Printed in green on re-verse "THE WANAMAKER STORE,/ PHILADELPHIA/LARGEST IN THE WORLD/1861 - JUBILEE YEAR - 1911" with Buffalo mark. **(A)**

Private Collection

29 | White Ware: Hand Painted

Although relief-molded and printed decorations are the most commonly encountered types of embellishment on white ware, many forms were hand painted with ornamentation ranging from simple to extravagant. Professional china painters, employed by the companies that made the wares or by firms that specialized in decorating ceramics, did most of the work which is available on the market or in museum collections. Forms include some tablewares, pitchers, shaving mugs, and vases.

Simple bands, border scrolls, and conventional floral decorations are the most common because they are easily reproduced by the trained hand of the professional decorator. The shaving mug by the East Trenton Pottery Company, illustrated here (see 29.2), is a good example of this type. Names, of course, might also have been added. On shaving mugs a name was generally used for the purposes of identification. Larger forms, however, were often intended as presentation pieces.

Ironstone and semi-porcelain pitchers were well-suited for presentation because of their large size, with plenty of space to emblazon the recipients' names upon them, and because of their convivial use on bars and sideboards as containers to hold water for mixing with whiskey.

These pitchers usually have a heart-shaped panel on both sides enclosed by simple raised scrolls. The area outside the scrolls was often painted a plain color (pink, maroon) while inside the frame was the name and occasionally a date as well. Pitchers of the same form are also known with advertising messages in the panels. Distributors of alcoholic beverages sometimes ordered them as gifts for taverns to be used on the bars.

The most common hand-painted decoration on ironstone dinnerwares was the "Lustre Band and Sprig" pattern, also known as "Tea Leaf Lustre." The pattern, executed in copper lustre glaze, consists of a small sprig of leaves in the center with a band near the edge of the piece. Its popularity began in the 1880s and continued into the early years of this century. In order to achieve consistency in the painting from piece to piece, guidelines for the decoration were printed under the glaze for the painters to follow while executing the pattern over the glaze.

Many different companies produced "tea leaf" ironstone in both England and America. Despite this fact, patterns and execution were so similar from company to company that a dinner service may be assembled today from individually purchased examples made at several different factories in both England and America. Manufacturers of this ware in the United States include the Mayer Pottery Company, Beaver Falls, Pennsylvania; Cartwright Brothers, East Liverpool, Ohio; and the Wick China Company, Kittanning, Pennsylvania.

Exquisite decorations of scenes and animals in landscapes were also executed on white ware. Some of these are so beautifully painted that only the type of ceramic body distinguishes them from some of the better decorations on porcelain. Elaborately painted scenes on white wares are more rare than similar embellishment on porcelain.

29.0 Vase (color plate)
City Pottery Company (active 1859-c. 1880)
Trenton, New Jersey, 1876-1880
Height 9"

Molded, white earthenware vase with squared handles; covered overall with handpainted scene in overglaze enamels depicting snowy landscape at dusk with church. Mark printed in red on bottom is a shield with "STONE PORCELAIN" above and "CITY POTTERY CO" below. **(C)**

Private Collection

29.1 Pitcher
John W. Phillips, decorator, on blank by American Crockery Company (1878-1887)
Trenton, New Jersey, Dated 1879
Height 8¼"

Molded granite ware pitcher with overglaze decoration of two large drinking scenes in reserve on a pink ground. Scratched through black overglaze on bottom is "John W. Phillips/1879/Trenton, N.J." and underglaze printed in two lines "American China/A.C. Co." **(C)**

New Jersey State Museum

29.2 Shaving Mug
East Trenton Pottery Company (active 1877-1904)
Trenton, New Jersey, c. 1880
Height 3¾"

Cylindrical mug of molded ironstone with rounded, projecting foot and top rims, ear-shaped handle with molded ring around top; hand-painted white flower sprays on a maroon ground flanking a rectangular reserve with "J. Breining." in gilt. Printed black mark on bottom depicting arms of New Jersey with "IRONSTONE CHINA/E.T.P.Co." below. **(A)**

New Jersey State Museum

29.3 Pitcher
Greenwood Pottery Company
    (active 1868-1933)
Trenton, New Jersey, Dated 1892
Height 9½"

Heavy molded "sweetheart" pitcher of a porcelanous white body,
decorated in gold with a pink
ground and made for presentation to "Robert Adrain,/President
of the Senate" with the arms of
New Jersey in colors on the reverse. The Greenwood Pottery Co.
made fine art porcelain in addition to sturdier institutional wares.
(B)

NMAH

29.4 Wash Pitcher
Ott and Brewer's Etruria Pottery
    (1871-1892)
Trenton, New Jersey, c. 1890
Height 11½"

Molded ironstone wash pitcher
with low relief bow outlined with
gold on a painted magenta ribbon; ruffled neck. Used with wash
bowl, which is marked. **(A)**

New Jersey State Museum

29.5 Platter
Glasgow Pottery of John Moses
    and Sons (1895-1905)
Trenton, New Jersey, Dated 1900
Length 13"; Width 9⅞"

Molded ironstone platter with ser-
pentine edge; hand painted
overall with scene of woman in
white classical robes; interior executed in multicolored enamels
and surrounded by a border of
pink roses with green leaves.
Signed "F. RICKETTS/1900" at lower
left; printed mark on reverse
"ROYAL PORCELAIN/PSYCHE" in a
crowned circle above "J.M.&S.
Co." **(B-C)**

New Jersey State Museum

29.6 Plate
Mayer Manufacturing Company (established 1881)
Beaver Falls, Pennsylvania, c. 1890
Diameter 8"

Molded ironstone plate decorated with a cut sponge in a brown and blue floral pattern on the outer rim in style known as "stick spatter." Printed mark "MAYER MFG.CO." on bottom. **(A)**

30 | Porcelain: Eighteenth Century

Porcelain production in America began late and developed slowly. Although porcelain had been manufactured in Europe by the early eighteenth century, it was not until 1769 that there was a serious, large-scale attempt to make it in America. Circumstances here simply were not conducive to its successful manufacture until well into the nineteenth century.

Prior to 1765 there were several persons who claimed to have made porcelain in America; however, only one small bowl attributed to Andrew Duché survives. Duché, working in Savannah, Georgia, in 1739, said he was the first man in the Western world to make porcelain in the oriental manner. His experiments apparently continued until at least 1741.

In December of 1769 the potter Gousse Bonnin and his partner, George Anthony Morris, advertised the impending opening of their China Works in the Southwark section of Philadelphia. Their advertisement proclaimed, "that the clays of America are productive of a good Porcelain, as any heretofore manufactured at the famous factory in Bow, near London. . . ." At the time of the ad the pottery works had not been completed. They still needed skilled workmen as well as apprentices (twelve to fifteen years of age).

By January 1771 the factory was still in financial difficulty and the proprietors were appealing to the Assembly in Philadelphia for a, "Provincial Loan, at the Discretion of your Honorable House, independent of interest, for a certain Term of Years." Also in 1771 the proprietors offered a lottery in New Castle, Delaware, "for the encouragement of the American China Manufactory." How successful they were in raising funds is suggested by the fact that, late in 1772, Bonnin and Morris closed the factory and appealed for charity on behalf of the workmen who had been brought to America and were now jobless.

Examples of porcelain produced in this short-lived factory are quite rare today. In form, color, and decoration the ware is very similar to the blue-flowered artificial porcelains made at the Bow works near London. (Artificial, or soft-paste, porcelain is not made on the true Chinese formula, but includes a variety of materials such as ground bone and glass to achieve the white translucent appearance of true, or hard-paste, porcelain). Several examples of this early Philadelphia porcelain are marked with a handwritten "P" in blue on the bottom.

30.0 Sweetmeat Dish (color plate)
Bonnin and Morris (active 1769-1772)
Philadelphia, Pennsylvania, c. 1770
Height 5½"

Molded shell sweetmeat dish decorated with blue flowers; artificial porcelain. Although porcelain was made earlier in America, this company is the first for which a small body of work survives. **(E)**

NMAH

30.1 Basket
Bonnin and Morris (active 1769-1772)
Philadelphia, Pennsylvania 1769-1772
Height 2¾", Diameter 8"

Basket molded of artificial porcelain with pierced sides, flower-shaped bosses on the outside, blue floral decoration on the inside bottom; signed with "P"; originally owned by the Morris family of Philadelphia. **(E)**

Winterthur Museum

30.2 Sauceboat
Bonnin and Morris (active 1769-1772)
Philadelphia, Pennsylvania 1769-1772
Height 4", Length 7⅜"

Sauceboat molded of artificial porcelain with decorations in low relief; blue designs on outside and inside border; C-scroll handle; signed with small "p" outside base. **(E)**

Brooklyn Museum

31 | Porcelain: Empire

The emergence of the Empire style, which closely followed Greek and Roman models, coincided with the reign of Napolean I as the French Emperor, beginning in 1804. In addition to classical designs, Egyptian motifs were also popular. The style became fashionable in America by 1815.

In ceramics the most significant porcelains produced in the Empire style were those made by William Ellis Tucker and his successors in Philadelphia, beginning about 1826. Tucker's first involvement with ceramics was through his father's china shop as a decorator of French porcelain blanks. The small enameling kiln which the Tuckers built behind the shop soon proved insufficient for the experiments Wiliam wanted to perform in an attempt to produce porcelain in Philadelphia. Benjamin, the indulgent father, spent a great deal of money on these experiments, including the purchase of land in Chester County, Pennsylvania, and Middlesex County, New Jersey, to secure supplies of the proper clay. In 1827 their efforts were rewarded by the judges of the Franklin Institute in Philadelphia, who declared Tucker's product, "the best porcelain made in Pennsylvania . . . some of the cups and other articles bear a fair comparison with those which are being imported."

Financial problems, however, plagued the operations from the beginning. In 1826 and again in 1828, Tucker acquired partners to provide extra capital. Thomas Hulme, Tucker's second associate, was interested enough in the business to have his name included in the mark during 1828-29. Beginning in 1831, Alexander Hemphill gave his financial assistance to the factory (which was expanded). With William Tucker's death in 1832, Alexander's father, Judge Joseph Hemphill, took an active interest in the operation. Thomas Tucker, William's brother, was retained as manager because he had designed the new kilns and many of the patterns that were then in production. In 1835 the name of the operation was changed to the American Porcelain Company. The factory closed in 1838, a victim of the tariff controversies of 1825-33 and competition from lower-priced European wares.

The Tucker factory offered a range of tea, dinner, and ornamental wares including vases, pitchers, tea sets, coffeepots, and various plates decorated in overglaze colors with bouquets of flowers, scenes, and conventional repeating gilt patterns. Many examples which survive today bear marks identifying their origin. Unmarked examples, however, are difficult to distinguish from French wares made at the same time because the forms and decorations produced in Tucker's factory followed the French prototypes very closely. Phillip Curtis, in his article "The Production of Tucker Porcelain 1826-1838" (see bibliography), discusses several scientific methods which might be useful for determining the origin of unmarked examples. The fact that William Tucker may have continued to decorate French blanks serves to compound the identification problems associated with his products.

Several other porcelain manufacturers worked in America during the first half of the nineteenth century, but few of their wares survive. These makers include Dr. Henry Mead, a New York physician who founded a porcelain factory in Jersey City, New Jersey, from 1816-20; Abraham Miller, a Philadelphia potter who exhibited a "specimen of porcelain and white ware" at the Franklin Institute in 1824; and Smith, Fife & Company, also of Philadelphia, mentioned only in 1830 in the records of the Franklin Institute.

31.O Pitcher (color plate)
Tucker & Hulme (active 1828-1829)
Philadelphia, Pennsylvania, 1828-29
Height 9½"

"Grecian" pitcher molded of artificial porcelain and decorated in naturalistic colors with fruits on either side, conventional flower-and-scroll gilt decoration around neck; signed in red on bottom "Tucker & Hulme/China/Manufacturers/Philadelphia/1828". **(E)**

NMAH

31.1 Pitcher
William Ellis Tucker or successors,
**   the American Porcelain**
**   Company (active 1826-1838)**
Philadelphia, Pennsylvania
c. 1830
Height 8¼"

Molded pitcher of artificial porcelain; bulbous body with tall, outflaring neck, arched spout and scrolled, ear-shaped handle; hand decorated in reds, pinks, and greens with garlands, gilt bands, and scrolls; unmarked. **(D)**

NMAH

31.2 Pitcher
Smith, Fife & Company (active
**   c. 1830)**
Philadelphia, Pennsylvania
c. 1830
Height 7½"

Pitcher molded of artificial porcelain with squat bulbous body; tall, flaring, scalloped neck and relief-scrolled spout; hand decorated in natural colors with heavy gilding; written in red on bottom "Smith Fife & Co/Manufacturers/Phila". Extremely rare. **(E)**

Brooklyn Museum

31.3 Vase
Dr. Henry Mead (active
1816-1820)
New York, New York, and Jersey
City, New Jersey, 1816-1820
Height 9½"

Vase of classic shape molded in
artificial porcelain in two parts
with winged caryatid handles;
plain white. Dr. Mead was a New
York City physician who financed
a porcelain factory in Jersey City.
(E)

Philadelphia Museum of Art

32 | Porcelain: Victorian

Despite the successful manufacture of porcelain by several Philadelphia firms during the second quarter of the nineteenth century, the
major producers of porcelain between 1850 and 1875 were located
in New York, New Jersey, and New England. About 1848, Charles
Cartlidge, a native of Staffordshire, England, who for a time was the
American agent for the Ridgway Pottery, began production of artificial (soft-paste) porcelain in Greenpoint, New York. Pitchers,
tablewares, doorknobs, buttons, and a variety of ornamental objects
such as candlesticks, portrait busts, and plaques were produced in
Cartlidge's factory. Although the operation continued only until 1856,
the company won a prize for high quality ware exhibited at the
Crystal Palace in New York in 1853. The hand-painted Rococo-Revival
designs typical of Cartlidge's work include the use of the oak leaf and
ear of corn, as well as patriotic symbols like the American eagle,
shield, and flag.

William Boch and Brother, a nearby rival company, brought expertise from the German porcelain industry to America. Their most
famous pitcher depicts the figure of young Bacchus in low relief in a
setting with grapevines and a tree. In addition to pitchers, they also
made architectural hardware such as knobs for doors and furniture.
Their wares were signed as William Boch & Brother as well as Empire
and Union Porcelain. The most important period of manufacture by
the Union Porcelain Works was after 1861 and is discussed in a later
section.

Morrison and Carr opened the New York City Pottery in 1853. The
business, which specialized in artistic porcelain busts and ornamental pieces, in addition to earthenwares and ironstone, closed in 1888.
Prior to the organization of the New York City Pottery, James Carr had
worked for the American Pottery Company, Jersey City, and the Swan
Hill Pottery, South Amboy, both of which were producing Rockingham
and plain yellow wares. While still with the New York City Pottery, Carr
was involved for a brief time with the Lincoln Pottery in Trenton. Mr.
Carr experimented extensively in pottery manufacture during his
lifetime.

The chemists, Charles Kurlbaum and John T. Schwartz, began experiments in the manufacture of hard-paste porcelain about 1851 in
the Kensington section of Philadelphia. In 1853 the judges of the
Franklin Institute described their work as, "the best American porcelain we have ever seen. The body is particularly vitreous and in this
respect equal to the best French." The company, however, was out of
business by 1855 and few of their wares have been identified.

In New Jersey, the American Porcelain Manufacturing Company of
Gloucester attempted to produce artificial porcelain from 1854 to
1857. Few of the products of this factory survive because they had
great difficulty firing a successful kiln. Low relief molded pitchers with
roses or chinoiserie decorations are known. The factory continued
from 1857 to 1860 as the American China Manufacturing Company,
but was equally unsuccessful at porcelain production. Some artificial, or soft-paste, porcelain was also made by the company of
William Young and Sons, Trenton, between 1853 and 1870, in addition
to their manufacture of yellow earthenwares. The factory was purchased in 1870 by the Willets Manufacturing Company, which is discussed in a later section.

Clearly, porcelain manufacturing in America was still a fledgling
industry in 1860. Artificial porcelain made in America during the mid-
nineteenth century is creamy white in color with softly modeled low
relief decoration with overglaze colors used to some extent. Examples
of American porcelain from this period are rare.

32.0 Pitcher (color plate)
Unidentified Maker
United States, c. 1850
Height 8½"

Molded porcelain pitcher in the "sweetheart" pattern, exquisitely
hand decorated with flowers in naturalistic colors and gilt. Several
companies produced this shape. **(C)**

NMAH

32.1 Pitcher
William Boch & Brothers (active c. 1850-1861)
Greenpoint, Long Island, New York, c. 1853
Height 9½"

Pear-shaped pitcher of artificial porcelain molded with design of young Bacchus framed with grapevines and leafy scrolls, ear-shaped handle; impressed mark "W.B. & BR'S./GREENPOINT, L.I." on bottom. The same pitcher with gilded decoration is marked by Union Porcelain Works, successors to William Boch. **(C-D)**

NMAH

32.2 Pitcher
Charles Cartlidge & Company (active c. 1848-1856)
Greenpoint, Long Island, New York, Dated 1853
Height 12½"

Pitcher of artificial porcelain molded with relief pattern of corn on stalks; ear-shaped handle is corn stalk, also; gilt decoration of corn stalks near handle; floral wreath under spout enclosing name and date. Designed by Josiah Jones. **(D)**

NMAH

32.3 Pitcher
American Porcelain Mfg. Co. (active 1854-57)
Gloucester, New Jersey
1854-1857
Height 8¼"

Pitcher of artificial porcelain relief molded in chinoiserie design with mask under the spout; impressed mark "APM Co". Few of these survived the kiln problems encountered by this company. **(D)**

Brooklyn Museum

32.4 Cake Plate
Kurlbaum and Schwartz (active
c. 1851-1855)
Philadelphia, Pennsylvania
c. 1853
Diameter 9 5/8 "

Round plate of artificial porcelain
with paneled rim; hand decorated in natural colors with large
bouquet of flowers in the center
and four leaf sprays around rim.
(E)

Philadelphia Museum of Art

32.5 Cup and Saucer
Charles Cartlidge & Company (active c. 1848-1856)
Greenpoint, Long Island, New York, c. 1850
Diameter, saucer 7"

Cup and saucer of artificial porcelain molded in paneled pattern,
realistically decorated in each panel with flowers framed by gold. **(B)**

Brooklyn Museum

33 | Porcelain: Parian

Parian is actually porcelain that has not been glazed, but left instead in the biscuit form. The matte finish which results from this absence of glaze gives the appearance of the fine white Parian marble after which it is named. Because the surface is not smooth enough to permit the use of such articles for food service (except for pitchers, which were glazed inside), most wares produced in Parian were intended for ornamentation. Elaborate vases and sentimental figures were particularly popular.

The new statuary porcelain was first produced at the Copeland and Garret factory in England about 1842. English workers from this factory may have been responsible for the introduction of Parian to the United States Pottery Company operated by Christopher Webber Fenton in Bennington, Vermont, where many patterns were made from 1847 until the factory closed in 1858. So much of the Parian produced in Bennington was modeled after English examples, in fact, that it is often difficult to determine the origin of pieces unless they are marked.

Products based on English designs included pitchers with floral and leaf patterns; figures in various sizes of children, animals, or famous men; ornamental vases and ewers, including many with elaborate grape clusters, roses, portraits and figures in relief, and hands presenting shells of various sorts; and trinket boxes covered with shells or conventional designs, often with finials of grape clusters or recumbent children. A number of the patterns were executed with a blue glaze on the stippled background to give the impression of the blue and white jasper ware produced primarily by Wedgwood in England. The English also made such imitations in Parian, but the blue is not as brilliant as on the American examples.

Despite the pronounced tendency to copy English models, there were a few patterns based on American images. The corn pitchers and "Cascade" (Niagara Falls) pitcher, for example, are distinctly American in inspiration.

The manufacture of Parian was not restricted to the United States Pottery Company. Other porcelain manufacturers of the late nineteenth century also produced figures, pitchers, and vases with a biscuit finish, including Charles Cartlidge and Company and the Union Porcelain Works of Greenpoint, New York; Ott and Brewer and the Lenox Company of Trenton, New Jersey; and the New York City Pottery of Morrison and Carr.

33.O Pitcher (color plate)
United States Pottery Company (active 1847-1858)
Bennington, Vermont, c. 1850
Height 10⅛"

Molded Parian pitcher with acorns and oak leaves on a bright blue stippled ground; extravagant rustic handle; raised ribbon mark with letters "U.S.P." Christopher W. Fenton's factory turned out an enormous amount of Parian ware within a very short period of time. **(C)**

NMAH

33.1 Pitcher
United States Pottery Company
  (active 1847-1858)
Bennington, Vermont, c. 1850
Height 11"

Parian pitcher molded in high relief with ears of corn and rococo
husks; pear-shaped body with
neck and spout in the form of a
sauceboat; cornstalk handle;
glazed inside. **(C)**

NMAH

33.2 Mug
William Bloor
East Liverpool, Ohio, 1859-1862
Height 4¼"

Molded white Parian mug with raised decoration depicting bust of
George Washington and leafy vines; background tinted dark blue; impressed mark on bottom "W. BLOOR". **(B)**

33.3 Three Vases
United States Pottery Company (active 1847-1858)
Bennington, Vermont, c. 1850
Heights 2"-8¾"

Molded Parian vases that incorporate ears of corn and shells in patterns typical of the period. **(A-B, each)**

NMAH

33.4 Vase
United States Pottery Company
 (active 1847-1858)
Bennington, Vermont
1853-1858
Height 16¼"

Molded Parian vase with six large
vertical leaves in low relief; twig
handles and applied decoration
of grape clusters and leaves; unmarked. **(C)**

New Jersey State Museum

33.5 Figure
United States Pottery Company
(active 1847-1858)
Bennington, Vermont, c. 1850
Height 4¾"

Molded Parian figure entitled
"The Tight Shoe," shows a young
girl kneeling on a square pillow
while adjusting her shoe. The
sweet sentiment of this figure is
typical of the work of Christopher
Webber Fenton. **(B)**

Metropolitan Museum of Art

33.6 Portrait Bust of Franklin
Ott & Brewer (active 1873-1892)
Trenton, New Jersey, 1876
Height 7½"

Modeled by the sculptor Isaac Broome, this beautifully crafted bust of
Benjamin Franklin illustrates how closely Parian ware resembles the
marble for which it is named. Signed "Broome, Sc., 1876." **(D)**

NMAH

34 | Porcelain: Late Victorian

After the Civil War the American porcelain industry began to flourish. The expansive development beginning in the 1870s was, in part, a result of the recovery from the depredations of the war, as well as an outgrowth of the cumulative knowledge of materials, sources, and processes acquired by the American ceramic industry as a whole. The major ceramic production centers, principally Trenton, New Jersey, and East Liverpool, Ohio, continued at the forefront of the industry.

The Union Porcelain Works in Greenpoint, New York, became particularly important as a porcelain manufacturing company after 1861, when it was purchased by Thomas C. Smith from William Boch and Brother, mentioned previously. In 1874 Smith and his brother hired Karl Müller, a German clay sculptor trained in Paris. Many of the models fashioned by Müller for the U.P.W. have become monuments in the history of American porcelain, including the famous "Century Vase" and "Liberty Cup," in addition to a number of brilliantly conceived busts, pitchers, and tea services. A hard, or true, porcelain body and the use of underglaze colors were two innovations introduced to the American porcelain industry by the Smiths. The Union Porcelain Works survived into the early years of the twentieth century.

Porcelain was first made in East Liverpool, Ohio, by William Bloor from about 1860 until 1862, when he left Ohio for Trenton. The principal manufacturer of porcelain in Ohio, however, was the firm of Knowles, Taylor and Knowles—founded in 1870 in East Liverpool by Isaac W. Knowles, John N. Taylor, and Homer S. Knowles. Initially they made common yellow- and brown-glazed wares, and then white granite, or ironstone. In 1887 the partners brought Joshua Poole from the Belleek factory in Ireland to produce the exquisitely thin, creamy ware for which this Irish firm is still famous. After a disastrous fire in 1889 which burned the china works to the ground, Knowles, Taylor and Knowles began to produce their celebrated line of "Lotus Ware," a variant of belleek porcelain with a soft velvety glaze in contrast to the glassy, almost pearlized, glaze characteristic of the Irish product. Vases with floral decorations in pastel colors and gold, occasionally with openwork patterns, are typical of "Lotus Ware." Raised, jeweled effects were also achieved, as well as **pâte-sur-pâte** ornamentation produced by modeling fine white clay pastes over the glaze.

The Knowles, Taylor and Knowles Company survived until about 1928. While they are, perhaps, most noted today for their "Lotus Ware," their principal commercial lines were of hotel china. In 1890 the plant included thirty-five kilns covering ten acres. Twelve of these kilns were reserved for decorating wares.

34.0 Oyster Plate (color plate)
Union Porcelain Works (1861-1900)
Greenpoint, Long Island, New York
Patented January 4, 1881
Length 8⅝"

Plate molded from a porcelain formula similar to the oriental body, in a pattern which simulates oysters on the half-shell on a bed of leaves; used for serving oysters which had been removed from their shells, a typical late-nineteenth-century contrivance. **(B)**

NMAH

34.1 Two Vases
Knowles, Taylor & Knowles (active 1870-1928)
East Liverpool, Ohio, 1889-1900
Heights 9¾", 7½"

Knowles, Taylor & Knowles were famous for their "Lotus Ware," a variation on the Belleek body made by many other factories. These two vases, molded with applied decorations and hand decorating, are good examples of this line. Both marked "K.T.K." and "Lotus Ware".
(C-D, each)

NMAH

34.2 Two Vases
Union Porcelain Works (Karl Muller) 1861-1900
Greenpoint, Long Island, New York, c. 1876
Heights: left 8⅛", right 8⅜"

Jack-in-the-pulpit vases in two varieties designed by Karl Muller, who '
began working for UPW in 1874. These vases were also decorated in
brilliant colors on hard-paste porcelain; marks on both consist of im-

pressed eagle head with "S" located in beak. **(C, each)**

NMAH

34.3 Tea Set
Union Porcelain Works (Karl Muller) 1861-1900

Greenpoint, Long Island, New York, c. 1876
Height, teapot 6¾"

The late-Victorian taste for the exotic is shown in Muller's extravagant tea set of hard-paste porcelain modeled with heads for finials and birds and animals for handles and feet; the painted decorations were inspired by oriental models. **(E)**

Brooklyn Museum

34.4 Century Vase
Union Porcelain Works (Karl Muller) 1861-1900
Greenpoint, Long Island, New York, 1876
Height 21¾"

Fashioned by Muller for the Philadelphia Centennial, the lower bisquit panels portray vignettes from American history while designs in the diamond lozenges above show contemporary machines. Heads of American animals were also included. Mark is "UPW" with eagle's head. **(E)**

NMAH

34.5 Cup and Saucer
Union Porcelain Works (1861-1900)
Greenpoint, Long Island, New York, 1876
Height, cup 4⅝"; Diameter, saucer 6⅞"

Also made for the Centennial celebration in Philadelphia; the figure is of Liberty, the white relief figures are in the manner of Wedgwood; hand decorated with much gilding. **(C)**

Metropolitan Museum of Art

35 | Porcelain: Victorian, Trenton

The most active center for porcelain production in America during the late nineteenth century was in Trenton, New Jersey. The Greenwood Pottery, Ott and Brewer, Willets Manufacturing Company, and the Ceramic Art Company (now Lenox) all prospered as porcelain manufacturers in this city.

The Greenwood Pottery, organized originally in 1861 as Stephens, Tams & Company, produced ironstone and, later, hotel china. In the early 1880s they added art wares to their production lines, including "Ne Plus Ultra," which was copied from the English Royal Worcester with an ivory finish and gold ornament. The many different under-glaze and overglaze decorations executed at the Greenwood Pottery were inspired by a variety of sources from oriental to Rococo-Revival styles.

The most famous of the Trenton porcelain companies was Ott and Brewer (the Etruria Pottery). Organized as Bloor, Ott and Booth in 1863, the firm produced only ironstone until about 1876 when the manufacture of porcelain commenced. In anticipation of the Centennial Exposition in Philadelphia, Mr. Brewer employed Isaac Broome, an American sculptor, to design and model works in Parian. The most famous of these include the George and Martha Washington tea set, the exquisite bust of Cleopatra, and the extravagant "Baseball Vase" (formed of a series of baseball bats surrounded by three figures pitching, batting, and catching with the whole surmounted by an American eagle).

Ott and Brewer's attempts to produce true "Belleek" wares began in 1882 with the aid of the Bromley family from the Belleek factory in Ireland. The American ceramic historian, Edwin AtLee Barber, remarked of Ott and Brewer's achievement that, "the rich iridescence of the nacreous glaze is fully equal to that of the Irish Belleek . . . in delicacy of coloring and lightness of weight the Trenton ware is even superior." Ott and Brewer's belleek, made in both ornamental and useful designs, was typically decorated in patterns adapted from the oriental, with flowers and leaves executed in gold on shell, melon, and leaf shapes with rustic handles. The factory closed in 1892.

The Willets Manufacturing Company, founded in 1879, had begun, like the other manufacturers, with the production of ironstone wares. In addition to sanitary earthenware, plumbers' specialties, and opaque china, Willets commenced production of a belleek line of art wares in the mid-1880s with the assistance of William Bromley, Sr., who had also helped Ott and Brewer perfect a belleek body. The Willets product was generally similar to Ott and Brewer's in decoration as well, although the shapes are adapted primarily from oriental, Irish, and European Baroque-Revival forms. Tea wares with dragon handles constituted a very popular Willets line. Production at the factory ceased, however, in 1908.

Walter Scott Lenox used the experience gained from working at Ott and Brewer and, later, the Willets Company, to form his own Ceramic Art Company in 1889 as a partnership with Jonathan Coxon, who had been with Ott and Brewer also. They sought to produce a ware similar to belleek, but of a sturdier composition. Lenox's product is a warm ivory color with a glaze which appears polished rather than shiny. In addition to vases and tablewares, the Ceramic Art Company also made such fancy goods as thimbles, inkstands, candelabras, and parasol handles. Many of the art wares were designed by William Gallimore. Their overglaze and underglaze decorations were for the popular taste, but they also produced a distinctive carved bisque ware as well. The firm name was changed to Lenox in 1906.

All of the potteries mentioned produced wares "in white" for over-glaze decoration by amateur and independent professional china painters. Forms, therefore, may be found either decorated or un-decorated.

35.0 Pitcher and Vase (color plate)
Pitcher: Ott & Brewer (1871-1892)
Vase: Ceramic Art Company (1889-1906, now Lenox, Inc.)
Trenton, New Jersey, Pitcher, c. 1890; Vase, 1890-1905
Height, pitcher 6¾"; height, vase 7"

Both are molded of belleek porcelain and heavily encrusted with gold; the vase with enamel colors also. The Trenton porcelain makers were a close-knit group. Walter Scott Lenox worked for Ott & Brewer and Willets before founding his own Ceramic Art Company. **(C, each)**

New Jersey State Museum

35.1 Pitcher
Ceramic Art Company
   (1889-1906, now Lenox, Inc.)
Trenton, New Jersey, Dated 1892
Height 5"

Belleek pitcher with handle in the shape of two rabbit ears; carved in low relief around the body is the legend "Little pitchers have great ears." Made by Kate Sears for a friend who was originally from Kansas where jack rabbits are common. Possibly unique. **(D)**

New Jersey State Museum

35.2 Tea Set

Morris and Willmore (1876-1905)
Trenton, New Jersey, 1893-1905
Length, teapot 8¼"

Molded belleek tea set with teapot in the form of a dragon; deep cobalt blue with hand-painted pink flowers in white-ground vignette; gilt handles. All pieces marked in orange with tulip enclosing "MW" with "BELLEEK" above and "TRENTON" in ribbon below. **(E, set)**

New Jersey State Museum

35.3 Teapot
Ott & Brewer (1873-1892)
Trenton, New Jersey, c. 1890
Height 3¾"; Diameter 6"

Belleek porcelain teapot molded in overall pattern of bamboo with rustic handle and heavy gilt and enamel decoration. **(C)**

NMAH

35.4 Two-Handled Cup with Saucer
Willets Manufacturing Co. (1879-1909)
Trenton, New Jersey
c. 1890-1908
Height, cup 2¼"; Diameter, saucer 6¹⁄₁₆"

Belleek porcelain cup and saucer molded in a serrated rib pattern with simulated coral handles; typical printed mark of snake in the form of a "W" with "BELLEEK" above and "WILLETS" below. **(B)**

NMAH

35.5 Dish
Ceramic Art Company (1889-1906, later Lenox, Inc.)
Trenton, New Jersey, 1890-1900
Length 12"

Molded porcelain dish in the shape of a leaf; the exterior hand decorated with flowers in gold paste and tan and lavender glazes on a pink ground; purple palette mark. **(C)**

New Jersey State Museum

35.6 Urn
Willets Manufacturing Co.
(1879-1909)
Trenton, New Jersey, 1881-1889
Height 10¹/₁₆"

Molded belleek urn with ruffled rim and large gilt-scrolled handles; the body hand painted by J.T. Baines for the Trenton decorating firm of Samuel Sherratt; red and pink roses on a light green ground. **(D)**

New Jersey State Museum

35.7 Picture Frame
Ott & Brewer (1871-1892)
Trenton, New Jersey, 1883-1892
9" x 11"

This exquisitely molded belleek picture frame with applied lillies of the valley was modeled by William Bromley, Sr. (active at Ott & Brewer, 1883-1892), who had worked in Ireland previously. The frame was passed down through the Brewer family. **(E)**

New Jersey State Museum

35.8 Vase
Greenwood Pottery Company
(c. 1868-1933)
Trenton, New Jersey, c. 1883
Height 6⅜"

Porcelain vase with bulbous body and long cylindrical neck; matte ivory ground hand painted with red and purple flowers and gold leaves. Identified in purple on bottom with Greenwood Pottery mark in imitation of the English Royal Worcester mark. The art ware line was called "Ne Plus Ultra." **(C)**

New Jersey State Museum

36 | Porcelain: Modern

Art porcelain manufacture in the twentieth century has taken a variety of forms, from commercially made blanks for china painters to limited edition figures to unique studio productions by artist-potters.

The art of china painting, mentioned earlier, reached its first crescendo in the 1870s, a phenomenon which led ultimately to the American art pottery movement discussed later in this volume. Interest in this hobby has revived again since 1900, to the extent that many American and European porcelain companies have produced blanks for this market. A network of supply houses, publications, and local and regional clubs cater to this pastime. Examples of work ranging from fledgling amateur attempts to exquisitely professional, artistic achievements may be found.

Many commercial companies have specialized in china-decorating on the blanks produced by other manufacturers. The firm of W.A. Pickard in Chicago, for example, has been particularly prominent in this century. Begun in the 1890s on a small scale, the company was selling its products through more than 1000 specialty outlets by 1908. The firm is best-known for its gold-encrusted and gold-etched effects. Independent professional decorators have also produced excellent work.

Since World War II the taste for porcelain figures which originated in the eighteenth century has been revived. Indeed, several companies have specialized in human, bird, and animal figures for this market. The two most successful of these companies continue to carry on the porcelain tradition in Trenton, New Jersey. Cybis Porcelains was founded in the 1940s by the Polish artist, Boleslaw Cybis. While the early work was primarily religious in nature, their current production includes a wide variety of themes, such as the circus, storybook characters, and famous women. The products of Edward Marshall Boehm, Inc., established in 1950, reflect Boehm's early interest in animal husbandry. The company continues to specialize in limited edition sculptures of birds, animals, and flowers, and has produced a number of elaborate creations used by presidents of the United States as gifts to foreign dignitaries and heads of state.

Porcelain is a difficult medium for the artist-potter to control because the requirements necessary for porcelain to be well-made are more stringent than those for work in stoneware. Clays, workshops, and kilns must be kept scrupulously clean because any impurities become evident in the firing. The process of raising kilns to the high temperatures required for porcelain can cause numerous problems with glazes and shapes as well. Large commercial potteries can absorb the occasional losses which come with porcelain manufacture; the artist-potter working on a smaller scale has much more to lose. Those artist-potters who have persevered in the use of porcelain as their primary medium have produced some of the most exquisitely beautiful work in ceramics.

An excellent example of the successful ceramist working in porcelain is Adelaide Alsop Robineau (1865-1929), considered by many to be the best woman potter to have worked in America. A long-time resident of Syracuse, New York, Mrs. Robineau's early interest was in china painting. In 1899 she founded the magazine **Keramic Studio**, which has been a great influence on amateur ceramic decoration. She edited this journal until her death. After 1903 she turned to the making of fine porcelain as a result of the influence of Taxile Doat, a famous ceramist for the Sevres Company in France and, later, artistic director of the University City Pottery in St. Louis, Missouri. In 1911 Mrs. Robineau received the award for "best porcelain in the world" at the Turin Exposition. Her work, which reflects the Aesthetic Movement in the decorative arts, shows patience and an exquisite attention to detail, both in modeling and glazing. These characteristics are best exhibited in her famous "Thousand Hours Vase," nearly seventeen inches tall and covered with small figures of scarabs painstakingly carved from the bisquit.

Contemporary artist-potters working in many different types of expression include Rudolf Staffel, Herbert Sanders, Kenneth Price, Robert Hudson, Lucian Pompili, Richard Shaw, Adrian Saxe, and Donald Pilcher. The fine modeling of detail and the brilliance of color that is made possible by the use of porcelain are shown to good advantage in the works of these potters.

36.0 Vase (color plate)
Rudolf Staffel, b. 1911
Philadelphia, Pennsylvania, 1963
Height 5½"; Diameter 6¾"

Rudi Staffel began working with porcelain in the 1950s. He calls vases such as this one "light gatherers," since their forms take advantage of the effects of light on porcelain. **(D)**

NMAH

36.1 Vase
David Seyler, for Kenton Hills
Porcelains, Inc. (1939-1941)
Erlanger, Kentucky, 1939-1941
Height 8⅜"

Ovoid porcelain vase with oriental crackle glaze, hand decorated with the faces of women in pastel shades of gray. Kenton Hills Porcelains was founded and staffed by skilled potters and decorators who had been laid off by the Rookwood Pottery in Cincinnati. **(C)**

NMAH

36.2 Covered Vase
Adelaide Alsop Robineau
(1865-1929)
Syracuse, New York, c. 1915
Height 5⅝"

Cylindrical porcelain vase with yellow and green striated glaze and openwork cover. Mark is impressed "AR" cipher in a circle. (See also 48: Modern Studio Pottery) **(E)**

NMAH

36.3 Three Vases
University City Pottery (1910-1915)
University City, Missouri,
**   1910-1915**
Heights (above, left to right) 9⅜",
    4¹⁵⁄₁₆", (below) 6¹¹⁄₁₆"

Porcelain vases, two with exquisite
blue green crystals on cream yellow grounds, the third with the
figure of a peacock in low relief on
a blue gray ground. The University
City Pottery was organized as part
of the Art Institute of the American
Women's League (begun by E.G.
Lewis). Taxile Doat, director of the
pottery, signed the tall vase on the
left. **(D, each)**

NMAH

36.4 Figure
Edward Marshall Boehm, Inc. (1950-present)
Trenton, New Jersey, 1960s
Height 14½"

Molded porcelain figure of a Bobolink on the stubble of a corn stalk,
colored with non-glossy stains in blues and greens. The figural work of
the Boehm Company is quite naturalistic. **(E)**

New Jersey State Museum

36.5 Figure
Cybis Porcelains (1942-present)
Trenton, New Jersey, 1974
Height 13" (including base)

Molded porcelain figure of Sacajawea seated with her papoose and
decorated with multicolored matte stains. Cybis produces thematic
groups of figures depicting human, animal, and floral forms. **(E)**

New Jersey State Museum

36.6 Vase
Lenox, Inc. (1906-present; pre-
**   viously Ceramic Art Company)**
Trenton, New Jersey, 1930-1950
Height 9⅜"

Molded cream white porcelain
vase decorated on two sides with
raised pink flowers and green
leaves flanked by vertical ribs.
Printed green mark of "L" in a
wreath with "LENOX/MADE IN
U.S.A." beneath. **(B)**

New Jersey State Museum

36.7 Vase
Willets Manufacturing Co.
**   (1879-1909) and W.A. Pickard**
**   China Studio (1898-1937,**
**   now Pickard Inc.)**
Trenton, New Jersey, and
**   Chicago, Illinois, 1898-1908**
Height 14¾"

Molded belleek blank decorated
in multicolored overglaze enamels depicting fall landscape with
cows; decorated by the W.A. Pickard china decorating studio in
Chicago. Signed on bottom by
both the Willets and the Pickard
Companies. **(D)**

New Jersey State Museum

36.8 Mug
Willets Manufacturing Co.
   (1879-1909); blank decorated
   by Charles C. Morris
Trenton, New Jersey, Dated 1908
Height 5⅝"

Belleek porcelain mug hand dec-
orated with gold and red cherries
on a black ground; gold handle.
Printed mark of snake in form of a
"W" with "BELLEEK" above and
"WILLETS" below. Signed in black
enamel "CHA C. MORRIS/1908".
(B)

New Jersey State Museum

36.9 Tea Set
Pickard China Studio (1898-present)
Chicago, Illinois, 1925-1930
Height, teapot 6"

Four-piece tea set including teapot, covered sugar bowl, cream
pitcher, and tray; all molded porcelain blanks made in Limoges,
France, and decorated by Pickard with gold floral design etched
overall; printed mark "PICKARD/ETCHED/CHINA" on bottoms. **(B)**

36.10 Bowl
Wheeling Pottery Company
Wheeling, West Virginia, c. 1904
Height 2⅞", Length 4⅝"

The Wheeling Pottery Company
produced a line of wares similar to
Irish Belleek called "Cameo";
molded porcelain in low relief;
mark on bottom "The/Wheeling/
Pottery/Co." **(B)**

Brooklyn Museum

37 | Art Pottery: Rookwood

"Art pottery" is a general phrase which refers to decorative forms of stoneware, earthenware, or porcelain made since c. 1875 for aesthetic rather than utilitarian purposes. For the most part this class of objects may be distinguished from porcelains made for the late-Victorian taste by its link to the Arts and Crafts Movement in the decorative arts of the late nineteenth and early twentieth centuries. Proponents of the movement decried the impersonal nature of industrial manufacturing methods that concentrated on producing the most goods for the largest market. They hoped, instead, to rekindle the taste of members of the middle and upper classes for objects that had been individually handcrafted. The designation of "art pottery" as applied to characteristic wares made prior to 1920 follows these tenets. The commercial success of wares made to satisfy this taste, however, led ultimately to the manufacture in many potteries of ornamental forms by the same mass-production methods so hated by earlier aestheticians. Thus, the term "art pottery" is really quite vague because it has come to be used for the most beautifully thrown and decorated wares of the Rookwood Pottery, as well as the mass-molded florists' crockery made at the Hull Pottery.

Because there were hundreds of large and small factories that produced art pottery, it is difficult to classify them. Categories based on geographical location are used in this volume because many collectors wish to concentrate on wares made in their own region. At the same time, this method of classification offers the advantage of focusing on the most widely recognized potteries of the industry. Ohio has been used as the starting point in this classification because it is the birthplace of the Art Pottery Movement in the United States. The history of the Rookwood Pottery and the concerns of its founder, Maria Longworth Nichols, embody the nature of this movement.

Until recently, the most socially acceptable artistic outlet for women was handicraft. During the early 1870s painting on pottery and porcelain blanks became a hobby for many ladies of the upper class. Maria Longworth Nichols was one of the large group of wealthy women in Cincinnati who joined this craze. Her enthusiasm, however, and her desire to compete with her rival, Mary Louise McLaughlin, led her to organize the Rookwood Pottery in 1880 with the financial encouragement of her father. What had begun as an innocent hobby became the most successful of the American art potteries.

While the women of Cincinnati were experimenting with ceramic bodies and glazes, they visited the Philadelphia Centennial Exposition and were intrigued by the exhibit from Limoges, France, of pottery with impasto floral decorations executed in underglaze slips (colored clays rather than glazes). Miss McLaughlin, who founded the Women's Pottery Club in Cincinnati in 1879, is considered to be the first American to understand and duplicate the Limoges technique. Many of the art wares made in Cincinnati during this period were decorated by this method. Laura Fry, a decorator at the Rookwood Pottery, discovered in 1883 that the colored slips could be applied thinly with an atomizer. Subtly shaded backgrounds of subdued brown and yellow ochre slip, decorated with painterly renditions of flowers, fruits, animals, and portrait busts, became the Rookwood

"Standard" line, imitated by many other potteries, but never duplicated for fineness of execution or delicacy of color application. The great success of the brown standard wares at Rookwood led, in 1894, to the development of production lines with different background colors: Sea Green, Aerial Blue, and Iris.

Decorative architectural tiles were introduced in 1902 (the New York City subway was a major commission), and a few years later garden pottery was added. Generally, however, the Rookwood Pottery is known for the ornamental vases and plaques they produced. Over the years many different forms and glazes were developed to expand their markets and accommodate changing tastes. When matte glazes became popular, Rookwood introduced a special "Vellum" glaze (1904) which had a semi-matte, parchment-like finish, but which, unlike the usual monochromatic matte glazes, could be decorated with varicolored slips.

Although successful through most of its long period of operation, the Rookwood Pottery finally succumbed to financial problems and was sold in 1960. Molds, equipment, and other moveable assets of the company were purchased by the Herschede Hall clock firm and moved to Starksville, Mississippi. An attempt to market the pottery was abandoned in 1967. The collector should be cautious of purchasing modern copies made with old Rookwood Pottery molds, marks, and decorators' signatures.

37.0 Ewer (color plate)
Rookwood Pottery (1880-1959), decorated by Kataro Shirayamadani (1865-1948)
Cincinnati, Ohio, Dated 1895
Height 17¼"

Tall ewer of buff-colored earthenware, modeled trefoil rim and spout, underglaze floral decoration on shaded mahogany and cream yellow ground; impressed Rookwood Pottery mark and incised artist's cipher. **(E)**

NMAH

37.1 Pitcher
Rookwood Pottery (1880-1959), Albert R. Valentien (working 1881-1905)
Cincinnati, Ohio, Dated 1882
Height 6⁵⁄₁₆"

Buff-colored earthenware pitcher of bulbous body with high neck and arching handle; underglaze colored slip decoration of owl in tree with moon and clouds behind; gilt details and rim; impressed mark "ROOKWOOD/ 1882" and incised initials "A.R.V." **(E)**

NMAH

37.2 Cup and Saucer
Rookwood Pottery (1880-1959),
    decorated by Olga Geneva
    Reed
Cincinnati, Ohio, Dated 1891
    (five flames above "RP"
    monogram)
Height 2¼"; Diameter, saucer
    5⅛"

Molded white earthenware cup
and saucer with hexagonal rims,
slip decorated with floribunda
roses on a shaded salmon background; clear glaze overall; impressed "RP" monogram; "W"
(white clay), "590" (shape), and incised "O.G.R." **(B)**

Private Collection

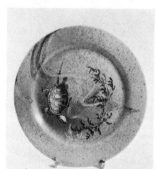

37.3 Plate
Rookwood Pottery (1880-1959),
    decorated by William P.
    McDonald (1865-1931)
Cincinnati, Ohio, Dated 1885
Diameter 6¼"

Molded shallow plate painted
with underwater scene of swim-
ming turtle and seaweed in colored slips against a shaded blue
green background; clear glaze
overall. Impressed mark on bottom "ROOKWOOD/1885/212" and
painted artist's cipher "WMᶜD".
(C-D)

NMAH

37.4 Paperweight
Rookwood Pottery (1880-1959)
Cincinnati, Ohio, Dated 1916
Height 3½"

Molded porcelain paperweight of a pair of geese on a rectangular
base; brown gray glaze; impressed mark of "RP" and flames with "XVI"
below. **(B)**

37.5 Vase
Rookwood Pottery (1880-1959)
Cincinnati, Ohio, 1895
Height 9½"

Molded buff earthenware vase of baluster shape; floral decoration
painted in underglaze slip on a brown background; overlay of sterling
silver openwork signed "Gorham"; impressed Rookwood monogram
on bottom. **(D)**

37.6 Vase
Rookwood Pottery (1880-1959),
artist William P. McDonald
(1865-1931)
Cincinnati, Ohio, 1898
Height 14"

Wheel-thrown earthenware vase crafted by the potter, Wells Sawyer; underglaze slip-painted portrait of "Chief Joseph of the Nez Perces" in various muted colors on the "Standard" mahogany ground. McDonald is considered one of the best of Rookwood's decorators. Indian portraits are the rarest and most sought after of the many kinds of decorations found on Rookwood Pottery. **(E)**

Metropolitan Museum of Art

37.8 Vase
Rookwood Pottery (1880-1959)
Cincinnati, Ohio, 1903
Height 8½"

Earthenware vase decorated with underglaze slips in various shades of blue with a prominent white sailboat and clouds reflected in calm water; Vellum-matte overglaze. **(D)**

NMAH

37.7 Vase
Rookwood Pottery (1880-1959)
Cincinnati, Ohio, 1899
Height 7"

Molded buff earthenware vase with portrait of "Three Finger Cheyenne" painted in underglaze slip on a shaded dark brown background; impressed "RP" monogram and flame mark, incised artist's cipher of "E.T. Hurley." **(E)**

37.9 Vase
Rookwood Pottery (1880-1959)
Cincinnati, Ohio, Dated 1907
Height 7¾"

Molded vase of white clay with
bulging shoulders and small
mouth; decorated with molded
and incised stylized leaves on a
matte-green ground; impressed
Rookwood flame mark and artist's
cipher "AFP". **(B)**

NMAH

37.10 Vase
Rookwood Pottery (1880-1959)
Cincinnati, Ohio, Dated 1920
Height 6⅛"

Molded vase of white body with
abstract lotus and leaf design
and olive green matte glaze; impressed Rookwood flame mark
with "XX" [ie., 1920] and "2140".
(A)

Private Collection

37.11 Vase
Rookwood Pottery (1880-1959),
    decorated by Charles Schmidt
    (1875-1959)
Cincinnati, Ohio, Dated 1924
Height 6¼"

Wheel-thrown, cylindrical earthenware vase flaring outward slightly toward sloped ogee shoulder; underglaze painted harbor scene in pink, blue, and beige with Vellum overglaze; impressed Rookwood flame mark and "1356F", incised "V", and artist's cipher. **(D)**

New Jersey State Museum

38 | Art Pottery: Weller

In 1872 Samuel A. Weller (1851-1925) opened a pottery in his hometown of Fultonham, Ohio. His early production was modest and consisted of utilitarian stoneware containers, redware flowerpots, and majolica umbrella holders and jardinieres. This enterprise was relocated to Putnam (now Zanesville), Ohio in 1888 where, after several more moves, the Weller Pottery settled down to a long period of success.

A figure who was instrumental in Weller's prosperity was William A. Long (1844-1918), an owner with W.H. Hunter and Alfred Day of the Lonhuda Pottery. Long had developed an underglaze slip-decorating technique copied from that used contemporaneously at Rookwood. In 1894 Long joined Weller in the Lonhuda Faience Company, but after Weller had learned the underglaze process he dismissed Long and proceeded to make the mahogany-colored art ware under the name "Louwelsa," adapted from his daughter's name, Louise, the Weller surname, and his initials S.A. The Weller factory continued to produce the Louwelsa line decorated with flowers and portraits of Indians, historical and theatrical personalities, and animals against the shaded brown background, sometimes augmented by silver appliqué to copy Rookwood's "Standard" ware mounted in Gorham silver.

The strong influence in America of the Art Nouveau style from Europe caused Weller to hire, in 1902, Jacques Sicard and his assistant who had come to the U.S. the previous year from Clement Massier's factory in France. Together they produced metallic lustre glazes on vases, boxes, and plaques with iridescent hues of blue, purple, and red. The "Sicardo" line was made until 1907, when its namesake returned to France.

The "Dickensware" lines made by Weller were also popular. The first of these was an underglaze slipware similar to Louwelsa, but with an unshaded olive green background. The second line had incised designs of Charles Dickens's characters, Indians, animals, and golfers hand colored with a matte or gloss finish. Dickens's portraits against a gray green background comprised a third line, which resembled the "Eocean" line of painted floral subjects against the same background.

After 1905 few of the Weller lines required much individual artwork. Weller relied more frequently on molded wares which could be colored by semiskilled workers, and this policy was quite successful. In 1905 it was reported that the pottery covered nearly four acres, with twenty-three kilns in operation and employing 500-600 persons. The bulk of production consisted of industrial art ware until the dissolution of the company in 1949.

38.0 Cream Pitcher and Sugar Bowl (color plate)
Weller Pottery (1888-1948)
Zanesville, Ohio, c. 1920
Height, pitcher 3⅜"; Height, sugar 4½"

Molded earthenware with low relief apples in natural colors on a cream white background; brown, rustic handles. Impressed mark "WELLER" on bottom. **(A)**

Private Collection

38.1 Vase
Weller Pottery (1888-1948)
Zanesville, Ohio, 1895-1918
Height 8½"

Molded vase of buff-colored earthenware having a baluster shape with underglaze slip-painted floral design and silver overlay in an openwork pattern; impressed mark "LOUWELSA WELLER" on bottom. **(C)**

38.2 Vase
Weller Pottery (1888-1948)
Zanesville, Ohio, 1897-c. 1905
Height 8¾"

Molded buff earthenware vase with incised decoration of Charles Dickens's characters in colors on shaded, matte-glazed green background. **(D)**

38.3 Vase
Weller Pottery (1888-1948)
Zanesville, Ohio, c. 1905
Height 10"

Molded vase with slightly bulging
cylindrical shape; shallow relief-
molded white narcissus and
green leaves on a shaded lavender ground; all in matte colored
glazes; "WELLER" impressed on
bottom. **(B)**

NMAH

38.4 Vase
Weller Pottery (1888-1948)
Zanesville, Ohio, 1902-1907
Height 9"

Molded earthenware vase of tapering ovoid form with painted
floral and leaf decoration in iridescent red, blue, and green;
painted mark near base "Sicardo
Weller". **(C)**

NMAH

38.5 Jardiniere and Two Vases
Weller Pottery (1888-1948)
Zanesville, Ohio, c. 1905-1930
Height, vase on the right 9"

All examples are of molded earthenware. Jardiniere is an "Art Nouveau" pattern with green matte glaze; wall vase has blue background with decoration in color; frog-and-lily vase is covered with "Coppertone" glaze in greens and browns. All marked "WELLER". **(A, vases; B, jardiniere)**

NMAH

38.6 Vase
Weller Pottery (1888-1948)
Zanesville, Ohio, c. 1905
Height 7¾"

Molded earthenware vase with snake at base and a frog on the shoulder, all covered in a matte green glaze; impressed mark "WELLER" on bottom. **(B)**

NMAH

38.7 Vase
Weller Pottery (1888-1948)
Zanesville, Ohio, c. 1940
Height 6½"

Molded earthenware vase with handles; pastel flowers and leaves in relief on a white background; impressed script "Weller" mark. **(A)**

39 | Art Pottery: Rozane/Roseville

"The Clay City," Zanesville, Ohio, located along the Muskingum River, was host to an unusual number of important art potteries. The Roseville Pottery Company was among the largest of these firms. It began in 1890 as a stoneware factory in Roseville, Ohio, but by 1898 the primary operation was moved to Zanesville, although the original company name was retained. Throughout its subsequent history in Zanesville, the Roseville Pottery Company utilized a total of thirty different kilns and employed at least 325 workers.

Like Weller, the Roseville Pottery imitated Rookwood's "Standard" ware with shaded brown slip backgrounds. This "Rozane," later "Rozane Royal," art line featured artistic floral groups, animals, and Indian portraits. Another less common variation was the "Azurean" line, which had similar flowers painted against a shaded blue to white background. Other early lines developed before 1910 were: "Egypto" (1904), a typical matte green relief-molded ware; "Mongol" (1904), an ox-blood red glaze in the Chinese manner; "Mara" (1904), an iridescent art pottery to compete with Weller's "Sicardo"; "Woodland," with incised designs of flowers in gloss glaze against matte, stippled grounds; "Fudji," developed by a Japanese artist, Gazo Fudji, had enameled designs painted on a buff-colored ground similar to his "Woodland" line; and "Olympic," a scarce line which had black and white Greek figures stenciled on a red ground. The art director at Roseville responsible for many of these lines was Frederick Hurten Rhead, who in his work from 1904-1908 also created "Della Robbia," a very rare sgraffito design which vaguely resembled French cameo glass in technique.

Few of these early art pottery lines met with commercial success, and Roseville soon began to manufacture less expensive types of simple molded ware with a minimum of hand-painted decoration. The new patterns, which relied on stylish molded shapes, formed almost the entire Roseville production after 1915. Many of these were pleasing and could be sold inexpensively to the vast middle class seeking to decorate with the increasingly ubiquitous art pottery.

Harry Rhead, Frederick's brother, came from England to take over as art director after 1908. The "Donatello" line, which he introduced in 1915, was one of the pottery's biggest successes. Over one hundred shapes were molded with ivory-colored relief figures of cherubs in brown landscape friezes on the heavily ribbed background, stained green. After Rhead left Roseville in 1918, Frank Ferrell replaced him and contributed over eighty different art lines. Through the use of imaginative molded designs requiring a minimum of painting on a matte finish, the Roseville Pottery was able to achieve a prominent place in the industry with sales of $1,250,000 in their best year, 1945.

Foreign imports and increasing labor and production costs led to a decline after World War II. Despite revivals of several of the earlier popular designs in a new glossy glaze, Roseville's share of the market continued to decline. The factory was sold to the Mosaic Tile Company of the same city in 1954, when production of the art pottery ceased.

39.0 Vase (color plate)
Roseville Pottery (1898-1954)
Zanesville, Ohio, c. 1930
Height 7⅛"

Ovoid, two-handled earthenware vase molded in "Montacello" pattern with mottled tan glaze, brown and green band, and black and white abstract ornaments on shoulder; unmarked. **(A)**

Private Collection

39.1 Vase
Roseville Pottery (1898-1954)
Zanesville, Ohio, c. 1905
Height 14¹¹/₁₆"

Tall, molded cylindrical vase in "Rozane" line; decorated in colored slip with iris on a shaded olive green ground; clear glaze. Mark "ROZANE/WARE/ROYAL." **(B-C)**

NMAH

39.2 Vase
Roseville Pottery (1898-1954)
Zanesville, Ohio, c. 1915
Height 10"

Molded buff earthenware vase of cylindrical shape with vertical ribs and molded frieze of cherubs; all in ivory, green, and tan matte glazes; unmarked example of "Donatello" line. **(A)**

39.3 Vase
Roseville Pottery (1898-1954)
Zanesville, Ohio, c. 1916
Height 9½"

Molded buff earthenware vase; semi-matte, deep blue glaze with thick raised slip decoration of stylized flowers and leaves in green, white, and yellow; artist initial "C", no company mark. **(A)**

39.4 Vase
Roseville Pottery (1898-1954)
Zanesville, Ohio, c. 1935
Height 4¾"; Diameter 6½"

Molded buff earthenware vase with abstract molded design around narrow neck; covered in a semi-matte, streaky blue and green glaze; unmarked. **(A)**

Private Collection

39.5 Three Vases and Candlestick
Roseville Pottery (1898-1954)

Zanesville, Ohio, c. 1940 (left example), **the rest c. 1904**
Heights: 4½", 8", 3¾", 5¼" (left to right)

Molded buff-colored earthenware; from left to right, "White Rose" line; "Rozane Royal" slip-painted floral design; matte-green "Egypto" candlestick; handled vase is also "Rozane Royal". **(Left to right, A, B, B, B)**

NMAH

39.6 Vase
Roseville Pottery (1898-1954)
Zanesville, Ohio, 1944-1945
Height 10½"

Molded earthenware in "Clematis" pattern; two-handled vase with yellow relief flowers and leaves, shaded ground from brown to green; marked "Roseville/U.S.A./111-10". **(A)**

Ursula Marrolli Collection

39.7 Baby's Plate
Roseville Pottery (1898-1954)
Zanesville, Ohio, c. 1910-1915
Diameter 6½"

Molded plate with rolled edge, buff earthenware with white glaze and printed design of chicks, colored bands, and inscription "BABY'S PLATE"; printed "Rv" mark. **(A)**

39.8 Bowl
Roseville Pottery (1898-1954)
Zanesville, Ohio, c. 1917
Height 4½"; Length 9½"

Rectangular footed bowl molded of buff-colored earthenware with blue glaze dripped over pink; "Carnelian" line; printed mark "Rv" in blue on bottom. **(A)**

39.9 Basket
Roseville Pottery (1898-1954)
Zanesville, Ohio, 1935-1950
Height 9"; Length 13"

Molded earthenware basket in "Pine Cone" pattern, smooth oval form with open top, relief-molded pine cones, branch handle; all covered in semi-gloss shades of brown and green glazes; "Roseville" mark on bottom. **(A)**

40 | Art Pottery: Other Ohio Potteries

The early history of the Ohio art pottery development is a complex and fascinating one. Although the Rookwood Pottery overshadowed its competitors and is remembered for its artistic use of underglaze decoration, it was preceded by several other Cincinnati potteries which produced art wares.

Mary Louise McLaughlin was responsible for the first successful duplication of the Limoges faience in the United States in 1877, after her exposure to the display by Haviland and Company at the Philadelphia Centennial Exposition. She experimented on earthenware blanks made at the Coultry Pottery in Cincinnati, which had previously made mostly utilitarian yellow ware and "Rockingham." By late 1877 the Coultry Pottery was manufacturing a limited quantity of the new art pottery.

In 1879 Coultry hired a young artist, Thomas J. Wheatley, who instructed a class at the pottery in the new underglaze technique. Wheatley left his employer less than a year later and hastened to open his own pottery, T.J. Wheatley and Company, in the spring of 1880. His technique involved painting creamy clay slips onto damp pottery, the same method used by McLaughlin. When Wheatley attempted to patent the method in 1880, McLaughlin challenged and won her suit. Wheatley and Company continued their production until 1882, the same year in which his old employer, Coultry, went out of business.

Another early Cincinnati potter, Frederick Dallas, manufactured ironstone and yellow earthenwares, but by 1879 he too was firing underglaze slip-decorated pottery for the Cincinnati Pottery Club, McLaughlin, and Maria Longworth Nichols, who shortly thereafter started her operations at Rookwood. The Dallas Pottery went out of business in 1882.

Matthew S. Morgan, an English artist who was working as an illustrator in Cincinnati, also made a short-lived attempt to establish an art pottery. He collaborated with the local inventor of the clay pigeon, George Ligowsky, and Herman C. Mueller, a German sculptor who had been working for a local tile company. In addition to the Cincinnati-style underglaze wares, they produced some wares molded in relief in patterns inspired by Hispano-Moresque architecture, covered with dark blue glazes and gilded. Their efforts ceased by the end of 1884.

These important early developments in the art pottery field were the forerunners of what became an extensive industry in Ohio. Zanesville Art Pottery was incorporated in 1896 as a manufacturer of roofing tiles, but by 1900 they were selling art pottery and had 100 employees by the following year. Their production included some popular imitations of other pottery lines such as "La Moro," a typical underglaze-decorated ware with shaded brown backgrounds.

Other notable Zanesville manufacturers include Peters and Reed, who produced art pottery from 1901-1920. After John Peters's retirement in 1921, Adam Reed changed the firm's name to The Zane Pottery Company. In 1941 the firm changed hands to become Gonder Ceramic Arts, Inc., (1941-1957). The A.E. Hull Pottery Company began production of art pottery in 1917 and specialized in an inexpensive line sold to gift shops and florists all over the United States. By 1937 the Hull Company could fill a contract for 11,000,000 pieces to a single New York distributor. Kitchenware, lamps, and several lines of art ware were mass-produced.

40.0 Vase (color plate)
Zane Pottery (1920-1941)
Zanesville, Ohio, c. 1925
Height 4"; Diameter 5⅛"

Round vase of molded red earthenware with dripping green, yellow, and black slips, all covered in a clear glaze; unmarked. **(A)**

Private Collection

40.1 Vase
Zanesville Art Pottery (1900-1920)
Zanesville, Ohio, c. 1910
Height 8"

Molded "pillow-shaped" vase of buff earthenware with underglaze slip-painted head of an Irish setter on brown background; impressed "La Moro" mark. **(C)**

40.2 Jardiniere
Peters and Reed Pottery (1897-1921)
South Zanesville, Ohio, c. 1910
Height 5½"

Round, molded jardiniere of red earthenware with relief design of pine cones and branches washed overall with a green stain; unmarked; "Moss Aztec" line. **(A)**

40.3 Vase
Dallas Pottery (produced art pottery 1879-1882)
Cincinnati, Ohio, 1879-1882
Height 7½"

Bulbous vase molded of a white clay body and tapered at the neck, covered in cobalt blue glaze with floral decoration of colored enamels in the "Cincinnati faience" style; impressed "DALLAS" on bottom. **(D)**

40.4 Mug
Avon Pottery (1886-1888)
Cincinnati, Ohio, 1886-1888
Height 4¾"

Wheel-thrown mug of white Kentucky clay with molded and applied "ram's horn" handle, shaded on the exterior in a dusty rose color with clear glaze overall. **(B)**

NMAH

40.5 Vase
Lonhuda Pottery (1892-1896)
Steubenville, Ohio, Dated 1893
Height 4½"

Round, squat vase molded with ruffled rim; decorated with yellow violets in underglaze slip on a brown background, clear glaze overall; impressed mark of date, and incised cipher of artist Sarah McLaughlin on bottom. **(C)**

NMAH

40.6 Pair of Vases
Matt Morgan Art Pottery (1882-1884)
Cincinnati, Ohio, 1882-1884
Height 19"

Pair of large ovoid vases of molded earthenware with flared necks and "pistol grip" handles; decorated and signed by N.J. Hirschfield in blue glaze with slip-painted yellow and white flowers and gilt trim; impressed mark and paper label on bottom. **(E, each)**

NMAH

40.7 Vase
Cambridge Art Pottery (c. 1895-1910)
Cambridge, Ohio, Dated 1902
Height 24"

Molded vase of buff-colored earthenware and baluster shape with slip-painted decoration of George Washington against a dark brown ground; printed mark "CAP" cipher in an acorn, "Cambridge", and "A. Williams/1902". **(E)**

40.8 Group of Three Vases
J.B. Owens Pottery Company (1897-1907)
Zanesville, Ohio, c. 1905
Heights 10¼", 4", 6½" (left to right)

Group of three molded vases, Left: slip-painted floral design, matte finish; Center: a molded dragonfly on rim, matte lavender glaze; Right: "Utopian" ware with slip-painted flowers on a dark brown ground. Impressed "OWENS" mark. **(B, each)**

NMAH

40.9 Two Vases
Wheatley Pottery Company (1903-c. 1910)
Cincinnati, Ohio, c. 1905
Heights 12¾", 14⅛"

Simple, molded earthenware vases, Left: green metallic spots on dark green ground; Right: deep gray green mottled glaze. Both marked with paper labels. **(C, each)**

NMAH

40.10 Vase
Clewell Metal Art, Charles W.
Clewell (1906-c. 1960)
Canton, Ohio, c. 1920
Height 5⅞"; Diameter 5⅜"

Globular earthenware vase, possibly a blank by Weller, covered with a thin copper "skin" on the exterior and patinated in brown and green; incised mark on bottom "Clewell/470." **(B)**

Private Collection

40.11 Vase
Charles W. Clewell (working 1906-c. 1960)
Canton, Ohio, c. 1915
Height 10"

Ovoid vase of molded earthenware with thinly applied coating of copper on the exterior; blue green patination; incised mark "CLEWELL" on bottom. **(B)**

40.12 Figurine
R. Guy Cowan Pottery (c. 1920-1931)
Rocky River, Ohio, c. 1925
Height 9½"

Molded earthenware figure of a dancer with colored enamel glazes; impressed "COWAN/RG" mark. **(B)**

40.13 Candleholder
Cowan Pottery (1912-1931)
Cleveland and Rocky River, Ohio, c. 1920
Height 3½"

Baluster candleholder molded of white clay and covered in a lavender lustre glaze; black printed mark "COWAN/RG." **(A)**

40.14 Figurine
R. Guy Cowan Pottery (c. 1920-1931)
Rocky River, Ohio, 1927
Height 10"

Molded figure of white porcelanous body depicting a Russian peasant playing a stringed instrument; clear crackle glaze; designed by Alexander Blazys; impressed "COWAN/RG" mark. **(B)**

40.15 Teapot
Nelson McCoy Pottery (1910-present)
Roseville and Zanesville, Ohio c. 1925-30
Height 7½"

Molded earthenware teapot and cover; cream white background, relief-molded ivy in green, brown branch handle; marked "Mc-Coy/USA/666." **(A)**

Matthew Wade Collection

40.16 Jardiniere
J.W. McCoy Pottery (1899-1911)
Roseville, Ohio, c. 1910
Height 5½"

Bulbous jardiniere of molded buff earthenware with slip-painted underglaze floral decoration on a dark brown and green ground; marked on bottom "LOY-NEL-ART". **(A)**

40.17 Vase
A.E. Hull Pottery Company
  (1905-present)
Crooksville, Ohio, c. 1940
Height 7½"

Molded buff-colored earthenware vase with handles and relief-
molded green and white floral design on shaded pastel ground;
marked "Hull Art/U.S.A." **(A)**

Ursula Marrolli Collection

41 | Art Pottery: New England

As might be expected, the Boston area was the center of the New
England art pottery industry. One of the most fascinating of the American potteries was started in 1865 at Chelsea, Massachusetts, by Alexander W. Robertson for the manufacture of utilitarian wares. In 1872
James Robertson and his sons Alexander, Hugh, and George formed
the Chelsea Keramic Art Works, and by 1875 were producing "antique" Greek terra cotta vases and urns. The redware was eliminated,
however, when production began on faience decorated with a variety of simple oriental and ornate Victorian designs in a wide range of
colored glazes. Some plain pieces sold to amateur pottery painters
should not be mistaken for the decorative work of this firm.

In 1880 James died, and his son Alexander left for California a few
years later. This marked the end of the typical commercial art ware
manufactured at Chelsea. Hugh C. Robertson had become fascinated with the exhibits of oriental ceramics at the Philadelphia Centennial Exposition. After assuming control of the pottery in 1884, he
began to conduct an extensive search for the secret of the Chinese
sang-de-boef, or ox-blood red, glaze which he perfected in 1888. During experimentation many other fine colored glazes were also developed.

The great cost of all this trial-and-error production was too much for the firm to bear. It closed in 1889, but reopened in 1891 to manufacture commercial tableware featuring the Chinese white crackle glaze that Hugh had rediscovered. A variety of designs in cobalt blue were used, the most popular being the rabbit pattern, a wide border of stylized rabbits and plants in a row. In 1895 the firm name was changed to Dedham Pottery when the factory was moved to Dedham, Massachusetts. Over fifty patterns of dinnerware were produced in subsequent years, while the art ware consisted of flambé and heavy, dripping "volcanic" glazes on high-fired stoneware bodies. In 1943 the Dedham Pottery closed due to rising costs and a shortage of skilled workers.

The other major New England art pottery was the Grueby Pottery, which began in 1890 with the manufacture of architectural faience at Revere, Massachusetts. In 1894 the name was changed to the Grueby Faience Company when art wares were added to production. The matte glazes developed by William H. Grueby were thick and subdued in color with a deep green used most commonly. Shapes were inspired by the work of the Frenchman, Auguste Delaherche. The style consisted of chaste relief floral and leaf designs that were very compatible with the new Mission interiors.

Many other small art potteries were active in the Northeast. The concept of using a pottery as a rehabilitative institution existed here as in other parts of the country. In 1905, for example, the Marblehead Pottery in the coastal town of Marblehead, Massachusetts, was started as a manual therapy workshop for Dr. Herbert Hall's sanitarium patients. Arthur E. Baggs was hired following his studies with Charles Binns at Alfred University in New York. Simple shapes were thrown and then decorated with soft matte glazes in stylized floral and animal designs. In a similar way, the Paul Revere Pottery, named for its proximity to the Old North Church in Boston (made famous by Paul Revere's ride), served as an outlet for the wares of the Saturday Evening Girls' Club, which employed young working-class women of Boston and gave them an opportunity to earn money while helping to finance their education. Their products were chiefly stylized floral and animal designs incised on art ware and tableware for children.

41.0 Vase (color plate)
Marblehead Pottery (1904-1936)
Marblehead, Massachusetts, c. 1910
Height 13 1/8 "

Wheel-thrown cylindrical vase of reddish earthenware decorated with stylized flowers in yellow, green, blue, and brown on a speckled mustard yellow background; impressed mark of ship flanked by "M" and "P". **(E)**

Private Collection

41.1 Vase
Marblehead Pottery (1904-1936)
Marblehead, Massachusetts
c. 1910
Height 3¾"

Squat, wheel-thrown earthenware vase with abstract floral design in brown, green, orange, and blue on a mustard yellow matte ground; impressed mark of ship flanked by "M" and "P" on bottom. **(C)**

NMAH

41.2 Teapot
Chelsea Keramic Art Works
(1872-1889)
Chelsea, Massachusetts, c. 1880
Height 7"

Round molded teapot with flattened sides and molded bamboo handle; raised design of birds and bamboo on sides; all covered in a glossy olive green glaze; impressed "CKAW". **(D)**

NMAH

41.3 Pilgrim Bottle-Vase
Chelsea Keramic Art Works
(1872-1889)
Chelsea, Massachusetts, c. 1880
Height 8¾"

Molded earthenware vase in the form of a pilgrim bottle, with low relief design of horseman calling the hunt; covered with glossy, olive green glaze. **(D)**

NMAH

41.4 Vase
Dedham Pottery (1895-1943)
Dedham, Massachusetts, c. 1900
Height 6"

Wheel-thrown white stoneware vase covered with Chinese "ox blood" streaky glaze; incised "Dedham/Pottery" mark. **(E)**

41.5 Two Plates
Dedham Pottery (1895-1943)
Dedham, Massachusetts, c. 1915
Diameters 6" and 7½"

Molded round plates with an overall white crackle glaze and cobalt blue painted borders in the owl and elephant patterns; blue rabbit mark printed on reverse. **(B, each)**

NMAH

41.6 Vase
Grueby Pottery (1894-1913)
Boston, Massachusetts, c. 1905
Height 6¾"

Wheel-thrown vase of swelling cylindrical shape with shallow leaf, stem, and bud forms modeled around the sides; thick dark green glaze overall; impressed Grueby Pottery mark. **(C)**

NMAH

41.7 Lamp Base
Merrimac Ceramic Company
(1897-1901)
Newburyport, Massachusetts
September 1900-August 1901
Height 8⅜" (with electrical
attachments 20¾")

Bulbous earthenware base with six loop handles on shoulder, covered with glossy dark green glaze; paper label on bottom. Tile and florists' crockery were the products of this company until art wares were added in 1900. In 1902 the name was changed to Merrimac Pottery Company. The company operated until a disastrous fire terminated the business in 1908. **(B)**

NMAH

41.8 Vase
Walley Pottery, William J. Walley (1898-1919)
West Sterling, Massachusetts, c. 1914
Height 6½"

Wheel-thrown globular vase of red earthenware with narrow neck and flaring mouth; covered in a thick green dripping glaze over a brown ground; impressed "WJW" mark. **(C)**

41.9 Vase
Paul Revere Pottery
Boston (1908-1915) and
Brighton (1915-1942), Massa-
chusetts, c. 1915
Height 9"

Wheel-thrown ovoid vase with incised band of conventional flowers; glazed white at the top against an overall blue glaze. **(B)**

NMAH

41.10 Three Vases and a Bowl
Hampshire Pottery (1871-1923)
Keene, New Hampshire, c. 1910
Height, tallest vase 11 7/8"

Molded and modeled vases and bowl of semi-porcelaneous white
clay, all with crackled matte glaze in green, blue, and tan; impressed
"Hampshire" marks. **(A, each)**

NMAH

41.11 Pitcher
Wannopee Pottery (1892-1903)
New Milford, Connecticut
c. 1900
Height 8¼"

Molded pitcher of buff earthenware with long, ear-shaped handle; streaked green and blue with
clear glaze overall; impressed
"W" in a sunburst mark on bottom.
(A)

Private Collection

42 | Art Pottery: New York State

Some of the earliest and most sophisticated experiments in the field of art pottery took place in New York State, although the rarity of the pieces today has led to omissions in the available literature. Charles Volkmar, like other American artists, was intrigued by the French display of underglaze-decorated pottery at the Philadelphia Centennial Exposition. He traveled to France and joined other painters who were working in that technique at the potteries of Theodore Deck in Paris and Haviland at Limoges. In 1879 he returned to the United States and established his own pottery at Greenpoint, New York.

An Englishman, John Bennett—who was the former director of faience decoration at Doulton and Company, Lambeth, England—came to the United States in 1876. He settled in New York City and built his first kiln on Lexington Avenue. After relying on imported English blanks for a short time, he began to produce his own cream-colored body and, to a lesser extent, a white body from New Jersey clay. Bennett's shapes were simple plaques and vases, but the decoration consisted of elaborate, painted faience floral designs similar to those made by Doulton.

Art wares in the French Limoges style were also made by Odell and Booth Brothers at Tarrytown, New York, beginning in January 1881. The production in 1882 featured faience umbrella stands; plaques with designs of landscapes, animals, and birds; vases; oil lamps and fonts; and tiles. In the same year the firm won the silver medal at the Mechanic's Fair in Boston, but by 1885 the business had folded.

Louis Comfort Tiffany, the renowned American designer of Art Nouveau glass, also created many designs for art pottery made at his Corona, New York, factory. This pottery was exhibited by 1904 at the St. Louis World's Fair and first sold commercially at Tiffany and Company's new Fifth Avenue building in September, 1905. Most of these wares were naturalistic with molded patterns based on American plants. Glazes were primarily matte ivory or green, although some pieces were left unglazed or had an iridescent surface. An unusual "Bronze Pottery" was plated on the outside with bronze and then artificially patinated for rich effect. Tiffany's art pottery was never produced in large quantity and manufacture ceased by 1914.

42.0 Group of Three Vases (color plate)
Tiffany Furnaces Favrile Pottery (1904-c. 1915)
Corona, New York, c. 1905
Height, vase at left 10"

Molded vases of high-fired white stoneware with a variety of naturalistic floral and leaf designs executed with yellow and "old ivory" glazes; incised "LCT" cipher on bottoms. **(D-E, each)**

NMAH

42.1 Two Vases
Tiffany Furnaces Favrile Pottery (1904-c. 1915)
Corona, New York, c. 1905
Height 12¾"

Two molded vases with baluster shape and designs of narcissus
winding around the sides.   Example on left is unglazed on the exterior with glossy olive green interior.   The vase on the right has a
grass green semi-matte glaze. **(E, each)**

NMAH

42.2 Vase
Faience Manufacturing Co. (1880-1892)
Greenpoint, New York, c. 1880
Height 13"

Molded vase of white clay; bulbous at base with long, narrow neck;
decorated with roses painted in colored enamels; impressed "FMCo"
mark. **(C)**

42.3 Vase
Graham Pottery (1880-c. 1903)
Brooklyn, New York, c. 1890
Height 7⅜"

Wheel-thrown, salt-glazed stoneware vase with acid-etched design of
deer-hunting scene which appears light in color against the dark salt
glaze; impressed mark "CHAS. GRAHAM/PAT⁰ APRIL 7TH/1885". **(E)**

42.4 Plate
Volkmar and Cory (c. 1895-1896)
Corona, New York, c. 1896
Diameter 11½"

Round molded plate with painted
scenic decoration in underglaze
cobalt blue of "Fort Gansevoort./
Present Gansevoort Market N.Y."
(B)

NMAH

42.5 Vase
Middle Lane Pottery/Brouwer
 Pottery
Middle Lane (1894-1902) and
 Westhampton (1902-1911),
 New York, c. 1900
Height 7¼"

Molded vase tapering gradually
toward the base, covered with a
thick, pitted, black and purple
glaze over a light green background; marked on bottom with
impressed "M" under whalebone
arch. **(D)**

NMAH

42.6 Vase
Buffalo Pottery (1901-present)
Buffalo, New York, 1911
Height 8"

Molded vase with olive green clay body decorated with colored
enamels in elaborate, stylized Art Nouveau floral design; clear glaze
overall; printed mark "Buffalo/Pottery/Emerald/Deldare/Ware" on bottom. **(D)**

42.7 Pitcher
Odell and Booth Brothers (1878-1885)
Tarrytown, New York, c. 1880
Height 9"

Molded pitcher of buff-colored earthenware with scroll-shaped handle; applied, hand-modeled flowers in high relief, decorated in Limoges-style painted colors; impressed mark "O&BB" on bottom. **(B)**

43 | Art Pottery: Mid-Atlantic

The premier art pottery made in the mid-Atlantic region of the coastal United States was produced by the Fulper Pottery at Flemington and Trenton, New Jersey. Like several other firms, the art line of Fulper was preceded by utilitarian earthenware and stoneware manufacture dating back to 1860, when Abraham Fulper bought an existing factory in which he had been working. Upon his death in 1881 the pottery remained under the control of his sons.

In 1909 the "Vasekraft" line was introduced at the Fulper Pottery. Distinguished by a wide range of forms decorated from among hundreds of different available glazes, the pottery continued to be made of the same heavy stoneware body. Painted designs were used only on a limited line of boudoir lamps and bisque doll heads. All of the art ware was decorated with dripping flambé, crystalline, or overall matte glazes in the Mission style. One of Fulper's most unusual products was a line of lamps with ceramic bases and shades inset with stained glass. The Fulper Pottery was sold in 1930 to its superintendent, J. Martin Stangl, who changed the firm name to the Stangl Pottery. The art ware was subsequently de-emphasized in favor of table and gift wares, the most popular of which were their bird figurines based on J.J. Audubon's famous watercolors.

The Clifton Art Pottery was another of New Jersey's factories producing art wares. It was opened at Newark in 1905 by a chemist, Fred Tschirner, and William A. Long, who had been a founder of the Lonhuda Pottery in Ohio and an early partner of Samuel Weller at Zanesville. In Newark they developed two principal lines of art pottery. One was "crystal patina," a subtle crystalline sheen in green, yellow, or tan over a semi-porcelain body. The other, "Clifton Indian Ware," was first shown in 1906 and featured stylized adaptations of prehistoric American Indian pottery with painted and molded designs on the unglazed red clay. This successful line was subsequently copied by the Weller and J.B. Owens Potteries in Zanesville.

Other art potteries established in the mid-Atlantic area included several in Trenton, New Jersey. The Cook Pottery, formed about 1895, produced a line of floral, underglaze-decorated pottery and two lines, "Metalline" and "Nipur," with metallic and matte glazes to resemble ancient ceramics. The Mueller Mosaic Company of Trenton was famous for its range of fine quality faience tiles, but also for an art line with marbleized glaze.

In Baltimore the Edwin Bennett Pottery Company, organized by 1845 for the production of Rockingham wares, introduced in 1895 the "Albion" line of vases comprised of lightly tinted clays decorated with underglaze slip-painted oriental and desert scenes. Production expenses and a lack of public response resulted in the Bennett Pottery being discontinued by 1900.

43.0 Vase (color plate)
Fulper Pottery Company (1909-c. 1930)
Flemington and Trenton, New Jersey, c. 1912
Height 7⁵⁄₁₆"

Round molded vase with two integral handles connecting the shoulder with the top rim; covered in a green crystalline glaze; marked "FULPER" on the bottom. **(B)**

NMAH

43.1 Vase
**Fulper Pottery Company
(1909-c. 1930)**
**Flemington and Trenton, New
Jersey, c. 1915**
Height 11"

Tall, molded cylindrical vase tapering towards the top with two flat, open handles squared at the rim; covered in a green crystalline glaze over olive green and tan; paper label "Panama Pacific 1915 highest award" (for the Fulper display). **(D)**

NMAH

43.2 Vase
Clifton Art Pottery (1905-1911)
Newark, New Jersey, 1905-1911
Height 6⅛"; Diameter 8½"

Round, molded "Indian Ware"
vase with wide bottom and smaller cylindrical neck; black, brown,
and tan matte glazes in a design
adapted from historic Homolobi
Pueblo, Holbrook, Arizona; molded "CLIFTON" mark on bottom. **(B)**

NMAH

43.3 Vase
**Mountainside Pottery
  (c. 1915-1940)**
Mountainside, New Jersey
c. 1920
Height 6⅝"

Wheel-thrown, baluster-shaped
vase of red earthenware with
yellow tan glaze overall and deep
green glaze dripped over rim; incised "MP" cipher on bottom. **(A)**

Private Collection

43.4 Vase
Pennsylvania Museum and School of Industrial Art (founded 1903)
Philadelphia, Pennsylvania, c. 1905
Height 6½"

Wheel-thrown and modeled earthenware vase with shallow relief design of stylized flowers, matte green glaze; impressed mark of keystone
and oval with "PMSIA" and monogram of decorator. **(B)**

44 | Art Pottery: South

The Biloxi Art Pottery (Mississippi) was a true forerunner of the modern
studio potteries in that one man, George E. Ohr, was responsible for
virtually every aspect of production. Ohr had built his pottery by at
least 1883. He dug his own clays, developed a number of richly colored glazes, and threw on the wheel some of the thinnest, most extrav-

agant shapes known in American art pottery. His predilection for the eccentric (the span of his moustache was 20" or more), led him to torture the thin shapes of his vessels by twisting, stretching, and manipulating them to test the limits of his craft. His enthusiastic experimentation resulted in the production of many pieces which appear innovative, even today. In fact, his unusual molded and modeled wares—artist's palettes, shoes, hats, and vegetables—anticipated the "Funk" ceramists of the 1960s.

In 1886 Ohr worked for a short while with Joseph Meyer at the New Orleans Art Pottery and at the Newcomb College Pottery after 1895 for an even shorter period. Apparently, Ohr gave up his potting about 1906 to enter the automobile business and packed several thousand pieces of his ware in the attic where they stayed, for the most part, until their purchase as a lot by an antiques dealer in 1972. If Ohr was not the "foremost potter in America" as he claimed, he certainly was the most **avant-garde.**

Just as the Philadelphia Centennial Exposition played an important role in the artistic development of the art pottery movement in the North, so the World's Industrial and Cotton Centennial of 1884-85 at New Orleans served a similar influential function in the South. The Women's Department at the fair stressed the artistic and intellectual education of women. After the exposition the newly formed Ladies' Decorative Art League took classes in various aspects of handcraft and, shortly thereafter, the New Orleans Art Pottery was formed in 1886. George Ohr of Biloxi and Joseph F. Meyer set up this short-lived firm (it failed in 1890). Many women used the facilities to fire their wares for a local art pottery club.

In 1886 the H. Sophie Newcomb Memorial College marked its beginnings as a division of Tulane University and an institution committed to women's education. Ellsworth and William Woodward, who had taught students in the Art League and the Pottery, were hired by the college to organize an art department. A pottery was set up in a basement and, after a false start or two, Meyer and Ohr were hired to form wares which the women decorated. After 1894 decoration at the pottery fell under the direction of a young Cincinnati woman from the Rookwood Pottery, Mary G. Sheerer. Designs from the beginning consisted of incised and/or painted renditions of local flora and fauna. Until about 1908 wares were given glossy glazes. The famous Newcomb matte glaze was used almost exclusively after that time until about 1940, when a modern style was initiated and simple shapes with plain colored glazes were used.

There were a number of art potters concentrated in North Carolina. Juliana and Jacques Busbee began their Jugtown Pottery in 1921 and hired Ben Owen as the chief potter. At the same time that revival redware and stoneware were made, Busbee developed glazes for wares in the Chinese and Japanese manner. In 1958 the pottery failed and Owen left to start his own operation. Today under new ownership, the Jugtown Pottery has discontinued the art pottery lines and concentrates on the revival wares.

W.B. Stephen produced art pottery in Tennessee at the Nonconnah Pottery from 1901-1912, and then moved to Mount Pisgah, North Carolina, where he worked until 1961. Early wares included dark green matte-glazed pieces with raised slip designs of wagon trains and Indians. Later, plain glossy and brilliant crystalline glazes were used.

44.0 Pitcher (color plate)
George E. Ohr's Biloxi Art Pottery (c. 1883-1910)
Biloxi, Mississippi, c. 1895
Height 8¼"

Thin wheel-thrown pitcher of red earthenware with applied loop handle, twisted waist, impressed band of chevrons, and deep red glaze
with white spots and green highlights; impressed mark "G.E.OHR,/
Biloxi, Miss." on bottom. **(E)**

Private Collection

44.1 Two Vases and a Bowl
George E. Ohr's Biloxi Art Pottery (c. 1883-1910)
Biloxi, Mississippi, c. 1895
Height, tallest vase 8½"

Wheel-thrown vases and bowl in yellow buff earthenware with twisted and crimped forms; variegated glazes in green, plum, tan, and brown; impressed mark "G.E.OHR,/Biloxi, Miss." **(Left to right, D, E, C)**

NMAH

44.2 "Puzzle" Mug
George E. Ohr's Biloxi Art Pottery
  (c. 1883-1910)
Biloxi, Mississippi, c. 1900
Height 3⅝"; Width 5¼"

Molded and modeled earthenware mug pierced with holes and having a hollow handle and rim pierced on one side (from which to drink); covered in a glossy, deep brown speckled glaze. **(B)**

NMAH

44.3 Vase and Mug

Newcomb Pottery (1895-1948)
New Orleans, Louisiana, c. 1905
Height 11¾"

Wheel-thrown concave cylindrical vase and convex cylindrical mug
with applied ear-shaped handles; incised designs of "wild tomato"
and floral and leaf in blue, green, and yellow glazes with clear glossy
glaze overall; marked with incised ciphers and impressed "N" [enclos-
ed in circle]. **(D, vase; C, mug)**

NMAH

44.4 Two Vases
Niloak Pottery (1909-1946)
Benton, Arkansas, c. 1915
Heights 5½" and 4"

Wheel-thrown earthenware vases of marbleized blue, brown, and
white clays; glazed interiors only; impressed "NILOAK" mark. **(A, each)**
NMAH

44.5 Vase
Jugtown Pottery (c. 1920-present)
Seagrove, North Carolina
c. 1925
Height 10½"

Wheel-thrown, baluster-shaped vase of red earthenware in "Chinese Blue" glaze with deep red beneath; impressed "JUGTOWN/ WARE" in circular mark on bottom. **(B)**

Private Collection

44.6 Dish
North State Pottery (1924-1959)
Sanford, North Carolina, 1939-59
Width 5⅞"

Wheel-thrown and modeled red earthenware dish; round with squared sides and applied loop handle; yellow glaze with dripping green and red glazes and clear glaze overall; impressed mark. **(A)**

Private Collection

44.7 Vase
Pisgah Forest Pottery, W.B.
**   Stephen (1926-1961)**
Arden, North Carolina, c. 1930
Height 5¼"

Wheel-thrown, baluster-shaped vase of fine white stoneware; tan glaze with aquamarine crystals, the interior glazed pink; raised "PISGAH FOREST" mark on bottom. **(B)**

Private Collection

45 | Art Pottery: California

The first art pottery produced in California was a line of fancy semi-porcelain tea sets and vases made from fine New Jersey clay at the Stockton Terra Cotta Company in 1894. In the spring of 1895 they introduced the "Reckston" line, which consisted of underglaze slip-decorated pieces similar to the Rookwood "Standard" wares. The company was re-formed in 1896 as the Stockton Art Pottery Company and the spelling of the art line's name was changed to "Rekston." This line was made from a native California yellow clay. Other lines with plain and mottled blue, green, and tan glossy glazes were soon added, but by 1900 the company had gone out of business.

After Alexander W. Robertson left his brother Hugh at the Chelsea Keramic Art Works in Massachusetts, he moved to California in 1884. He did some experimental work with local clays after 1891, when he met the wife of the California state minerologist, Linna Irelan. Together they worked to establish an art pottery which, after several problems, opened in 1898 in San Francisco as the Roblin Art Pottery. The wares were thrown and glazed by Robertson while Irelan's interest and responsibility focused on the decoration. She utilized nearly every method popular during the period, such as modeled and applied lizards and mushrooms, underglaze slip painting, and incised or carved work. All clays and glazes used in the production were from California materials. In 1903 Robertson's son Fred joined the pottery, but the great San Francisco earthquake of 1906 destroyed the plant and stock, and production was never resumed.

The Robertsons left for Los Angeles where Fred worked for the Los Angeles Pressed Brick Company producing his own art ware fired in the brick kilns. He experimented with both clays and glazes and by 1914 was using crystalline and lustre glazes. After 1921 Fred worked at the Claycraft Potteries Company with his son George. The production of art pottery was limited to tiles, garden crockery, and lamps. Finally, in 1934 the Robertson Pottery was organized. Fine art pottery was made until 1952 at various locations in Los Angeles and Hollywood.

One prominent California art pottery was initiated as a craft center for women. The Arequipa Pottery was opened in 1911 by Frederick H. Rhead, who had been art director at the Roseville Pottery in Ohio. It was organized as part of the Arequipa Sanitorium for young women with tuberculosis to provide lessons for the patients. Rhead's pottery and the sanitorium separated in 1913, but after his departure in 1914, the two were rejoined with Albert Solon as director of the pottery. Local materials were utilized in the production and wares were sold to stores throughout the country. The young women were responsible for decorating the pottery. As a result of their relatively short terms at the sanitorium, a wide range of quality is discernible. Although the Arequipa Pottery won a Gold Medal at the 1915 Panama-Pacific Exposition, the company went out of business in 1918, a victim of the economic problems suffered during World War I.

45.0 Vase and Bowl (color plate)
Arequipa Pottery (1911-1918)
Fairfax, California, c. 1915

Height, vase 10"; bowl 2⅜"

Earthenware, the vase with a brown purple matte glaze; the bowl with a variable blue glaze in the "ancient Persian" manner. **(C, each)**

NMAH

45.1 Vase
Arequipa Pottery (1911-1918)
Fairfax, California, c. 1915
Height 8"

Wheel-thrown swollen cylindrical vase with carved and incised flowers around the top half and covered in a matte, blue gray glaze. **(C)**

NMAH

45.2 Vase
Markham Pottery (1913-1921)
National City, California, c. 1914
Height 6⅞"

Ovoid earthenware vase molded in "Arabesque" pattern and having a coarse glaze with random lines in relief; incised "Markham" and "6312". The pottery was located in Ann Arbor, Michigan, from 1905 to 1913. Numbers over 6000 indicate a California origin. **(B)**

45.3 Mug
Roblin Art Pottery (1898-1906)
San Francisco, California, c. 1900
Height 3¾"

Wheel-thrown red earthenware mug with decoration of hops and leaves in low relief, covered overall with a streaked, olive green and brown glaze; marks on the bottom include an impressed bear and "ROBLIN" with the artist's name "Linna Irelan" and "No 5" incised. **(C)**

Dave Rago

45.4 Vase
Roblin Art Pottery (1898-1906)
San Francisco, California, Dated 1898
Height 3¾"

Wheel-thrown red earthenware vase with baluster shape and impressed beaded line at shoulder; white slip decoration of flowers; impressed mark "ROBLIN" and bear, dated 1898 and signed by Linna
Irelan. **(C)**

45.5 Vase
Valentien Pottery (c. 1911-1914)
San Diego, California, 1911-1914
Height 8"

Molded vase with elongated baluster form and low relief flowers and
vines in Art Nouveau style; semi-matte mauve glaze; impressed "VP/
Co", poppy mark, and "Z21." **(D)**

45.6 Bowl
Rhead Pottery (1914-1917)
Santa Barbara, California, 1914-1917
Diameter 7⅜"

Wheel-thrown redware bowl having a medium blue matte ground
with decoration of pomegranates around the rim in low relief filled
with white; impressed mark in a circle "RHEAD POTTERY SANTA BAR-
BARA" enclosing the figure of a potter at the wheel. The Rhead
Pottery earned a Gold Medal at the San Diego exposition in 1915.
(C)

Private Collection

45.7 Vase
California Faience Company
**   (1918-c. 1930)**
Berkeley, California, c. 1925
Height 5⅝"

Molded red earthenware vase
with waisted form covered overall
with a medium blue matte glaze;
incised "California/Faience" on
bottom. **(A-B)**

Private Collection

45.8 Vase
California Faience Company (1918-c. 1930)
Berkeley, California, c. 1925
Height 4⅛"

Molded red earthenware vase with cylindrical form narrowing sharply
at the top; glazed with deep blue matte; incised "California/Faience"
mark on bottom. **(A)**

45.9 Vase
Stockton Art Pottery Company
**   (1896-1900)**
Stockton, California, 1896-1900
Height 8⅞"; Diameter 5"

Vase with ruffled edge, the whole
decorated with hand-painted
morning-glories and vines in
yellow brown and green on a
brown ground; impressed mark
on bottom "REKSTON" below a
double circle enclosing "STOCK-
TON/CALIFORNIA" with "S/A/P/C°"
inside. **(B)**

Nance Darrow

46 | Art Pottery: Colorado

There were not many art potteries in Colorado, but the few that located there are known for the high quality of their wares. The foremost of these is the Van Briggle Pottery, established in 1901 at 615 North Nevada Avenue, Colorado Springs. Artus Van Briggle started working as a student of Karl Langenbeck, the founder of the Avon Pottery in Cincinnati, Ohio, in 1886, but by the next year was hired by the Rookwood Pottery.

Van Briggle's artistic ability resulted in a promotion to senior decorator in 1891, and within a couple of years he was sent to France to study painting. The emerging Art Nouveau style fascinated him and sparked his interest in clay modeling, while the matte glazes of the oriental ceramics he saw in Europe's great museums intrigued him. The experiments he began in Paris were resumed on a limited basis upon his return to Rookwood in 1896.

Most of Van Briggle's work for Rookwood consisted of underglaze slip-painted floral designs for their "Standard" line, but a few pre-1900 examples exhibit the influences of his trip to Europe. Indeed, much of the Rookwood production after Van Briggle left in 1899 features subtle molded designs inspired by the Art Nouveau style and soft matte glazes, some identical to those on early Van Briggle productions at Colorado Springs.

The decision to leave Cincinnati was based on his severe tuberculosis; he hoped that a change of atmosphere could provide some relief. He soon married Anne Gregory, a young artist he had met in Paris. Utilizing the Colorado clays, Van Briggle began commercial production in 1901 and was rewarded in 1903 by two gold and several other medals for his display at the Paris Salon and two gold medals awarded at the 1904 Louisiana Purchase Exposition in St. Louis. He died of tuberculosis before the end of that exposition at the age of thirty-five, but his wife and others continued making pottery modeled after his designs and from original molds. The Van Briggle Pottery underwent several changes in management following a move to a larger factory in 1907, but art pottery is still being produced there today.

The earliest art pottery in Colorado was the White Pottery established in 1894 at Denver by Frederick J. White and his son Francis. Early production centered on Rockingham wares and common yellow utilitarian pottery similar to that made in England and Canada, where Frederick had worked at the Cortney Bay Pottery in St. Johns, New Brunswick. In 1909 the Whites changed their output to art ware and their firm name to the Denver Art Pottery. "Denver Gray Ware" was made in many forms with a semi-matte gray glaze, while other monochrome glazes were developed along with typical underglaze slip-decorated pieces. An unusual line featured different colored clays mixed together creating a distinctive swirled effect similar to that made at the Niloak Pottery in Arkansas. Francis carried on the work after his father's death in 1919 and production continued until 1955.

The Denver China and Pottery Company began making art pottery in 1901 under the direction of William A. Long, who had founded the

Lonhuda Pottery in Ohio. By utilizing local Colorado materials, he continued the underglaze slip-decorated ware common in Zanesville and Cincinnati; majolica toilet sets, jardinières, and kitchenware were also made. The slip-decorated line was still called "Lonhuda." "Denaura," a line of molded Art Nouveau pottery with matte glazes similar to those used by Van Briggle, was sold until 1905, when the pottery merged with Western Pottery Manufacturing Company. Long soon left for Newark, New Jersey, where he organized the Clifton Art Pottery.

46.0 Vase (color plate)
Van Briggle Pottery (1901-present)
Colorado Springs, Colorado, Dated 1916
Height 4⅜"

Molded stoneware vase with simple leaf design and covered with a deep blue matte glaze; incised mark of conjoined "AA" and "1916" on bottom. **(A)**

Private Collection

46.1 Vase
Van Briggle Pottery (1901-present)
Colorado Springs, Colorado
Dated 1903
Height 17¹³/₁₆"

Tall stoneware vase molded and incised with abstract linear design and glazed overall in a plum-colored matte glaze; incised date 1903, "Van Briggle" and "AA" cipher on bottom. **(E)**

NMAH

46.2 Vase
Van Briggle Pottery (1901-present)
Colorado Springs, Colorado
Dated 1903
Height 9½"

Molded and modeled stoneware
vase with stylized iris in relief, the
background in aqua and magen-
ta glazes with yellow flowers;
marked "AA/Van Briggle/1903/III/
161" with a paper label. **(E)**

NMAH

46.4 Vase
Denver China and Pottery
Company (1901-1905)
Denver, Colorado, c. 1903
Height 8½"; Diameter 4¾"

Earthenware vase which has
been slip-cast from a full-size mold
with relief tulips and leaves; overall matte green glaze; marked
"Denaura Denver" on bottom. **(C)**

NMAH

46.3 Vase
Van Briggle Pottery (1901-present)
Colorado Springs, Colorado, 1960
Height 6½"

Molded stoneware vase of bulbous shape with glossy black glaze
flecked with white; incised mark "Anna Van Briggle/Colo Spgs Colo"
on bottom. **(A)**

46.5 Vase
Denver China and Pottery
    Company (1901-1905)
Denver, Colorado, 1901-1905
Height 8¼"; Diameter at
    base 3⅛"

Slip-cast earthenware vase, "Lonhuda" line, slip-painted decoration of milkweed on a brownish
green shaded background; overall clear glaze. **(C)**

Brooklyn Museum

47 | Art Pottery: Great Lakes

The American art pottery movement has long been associated with a
number of talented women. Unlike their English counterparts who
were primarily decorators, these American ceramists started their
own companies and were actively involved in all aspects of design,
production, and marketing. Mary Chase Perry of Detroit, Michigan,
began, as many had, by china painting and studying art and ceramics in Cincinnati, Ohio, and Alfred, New York. In 1903 she founded the
Revelation Pottery with a neighbor, Horace James Caulkins, who was
in the dental supply business and had produced furnaces for dental
use. His new "Revelation" kiln was made for use by china decorators
and Miss Perry agreed to promote it while conducting experiments
on clay bodies and glazes.

In 1905 the name was changed to the Pewabic Pottery (although
Miss Perry had informally used a "Pewabic" mark for a short time
before 1905). The range of glazes kept expanding with continued experimentation. Iridescent, Persian blue, crystalline, and Chinese
glazes were all used. Her success led Detroit's Charles Lang Freer, the
foremost American collector of oriental art, to support Miss Perry and
collect many of the finest examples of her pottery. In addition, a
number of architectural commissions were accepted, making tile
production an important part of her business. She married William B.
Stratton, the designer of her new pottery building, in 1918. Her work
continued until she died in 1961.

The Chicago area was home to a number of art potteries that, like those in many other regions, began as producers of utilitarian ware and architectural brick and terra cotta. In 1886 the American Terra Cotta and Ceramic Company (also called Gates Pottery) was established by William Day Gates at Terra Cotta, Illinois, but it was not until 1901 that the "Teco" line of art pottery was made commercially. A wide range of modern angular and organic Art Nouveau shapes was designed by Gates and local architects, including Frank Lloyd Wright. Glazes were generally a soft, silver green matte, although tan, blue, yellow, and other colors were used by 1910. A limited number of excellent examples of crystalline glaze was exhibited in 1904 at the St. Louis Fair. While early wares featured elaborate shapes, the pottery was soon offered through popular decorator's magazines, like **The House Beautiful,** and mass production led to a simplification of style and lack of innovation.

Another art ware which was a secondary product in an architectural terra cotta manufactory was "Norweta," made by the Northwestern Terra Cotta Company in Chicago after 1904 (for a very short time only). An excellent crystalline glaze was developed there while other pieces were molded in Art Nouveau designs and covered in a matte green glaze.

47.0 Jar (color plate)
Pewabic Pottery (1903-1961)
Detroit, Michigan, 1918
Height 12½"

Earthenware jar covered with a black matte glaze over which has been poured a second glaze with iridescent green, blue, and gold highlights. Impressed mark "PEWABIC DETROIT" in a circle on the bottom. The jar sold for fifty dollars originally. **(E)**

Freer Gallery of Art

47.1 Vase
Pewabic Pottery (1903-1961)
Detroit, Michigan, c. 1905
Height 4½"

Wheel-thrown vase covered with dripping yellow glazes over brown glazes; impressed mark "PEWABIC" in a curve with five leaves above. **(D)**

NMAH

47.2 Jardiniere
Norse Pottery Company (1903-1913)
Edgerton, Wisconsin (1903-1904) and Rockford, Illinois (1904-1913)
c. 1910
Height 7¾"; Width 12⅛"

Molded earthenware jardiniere, an adaptation of an original from the Bronze Age in Bornholm, Denmark; overall green black, dull metallic glaze; impressed "Norse" mark. **(B)**

NMAH

47.3 Planter
Pauline Pottery
Chicago, Illinois (1882-1888) and Edgerton, Wisconsin (1888-1893; 1902-1909), c. 1883
Height 3¾"; Diameter 8¾"

Molded, buff-colored stoneware planter, creamy "smear" glaze, incised floral and spiderweb designs highlighted with silver and gilt; incised mark "SPRINGER." **(D)**

47.4 Chocolate Pot
Pauline Pottery (1882-1909)
Chicago, Illinois, and Edgerton, Wisconsin, c. 1890
Height 8½"

Covered pot of molded earthenware with underglaze slip-painted floral decoration on a shaded brown ground with gilt highlights; impressed mark on bottom of a crown enclosing the letter "C". **(C)**

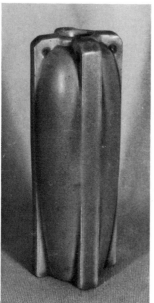

47.5 Vase
The Gates Potteries (c. 1890-1930)
Terra Cotta, Illinois, 1900-1910
Height 6⅞"

Molded buff earthenware vase with four angular buttresses, glazed overall in a silvery matte green; impressed "Teco" mark. **(B)**

Private Collection

47.6 Vase
Chicago Crucible Company (art
    wares c. 1920-1932)
Chicago, Illinois, c. 1920
Height 9"

Stoneware vase molded with parallel swirling lines and covered in a mottled gray green glaze. The firm specialized in high-fired industrial stoneware before it was acquired by the Northwestern Terra Cotta Company about 1920, after which, art wares were crafted intermittently with architectural terra cotta. **(C)**

Private Collection

47.7 Vase
Monmouth Pottery
 (c. 1890-present)
Monmouth, Illinois, c. 1930
Height 8"; Diameter 6"

Two-handled, urn-shaped vase of molded stoneware covered in white under a mottled matte green glaze; round "Monmouth Pottery" paper label. **(A)**

Private Collection

47.8 Vase
Red Wing Stoneware Company
 (1878-1967)
Red Wing, Minnesota, c. 1910
Height 7⅛"; Diameter 5½"

Molded vase of fine white stoneware with streaky semi-matte glaze in shades of yellow, green, and tan; "RED WING ART POTTERY" mark printed on bottom in blue ink. **(A)**

Private Collection

48 | Modern Studio Pottery

Distinguishing the studio potter from his counterpart in a commercial art pottery is not always easily accomplished by simply looking at the wares produced by each, since many craftspersons worked in both situations. Generally speaking, however, studio potters performed most functions in their own studios, as opposed to commercial potters, who designed, decorated, or shaped pots, but rarely accomplished all of these tasks. According to the classification of this guide, the studio potter is an artist who controls pottery production through several stages, including marketing under his/her own name. Art pottery, in general, is marked and sold as the product of an organization of persons with separate responsibilities.

A significant number of America's finest studio potters in the twentieth century have been women. Mary Louise McLaughlin (1847-1939) has been mentioned previously for her introduction of the Limoges faience method of decoration to Cincinnati and the United States in 1878. She worked at first in conjunction with several factories and clubs, but her later work reflected her personal experiments with different clay bodies, including porcelain. Another woman prominent as a studio potter, but who had worked with art potteries during her career, was Adelaide Alsop Robineau (1865-1929). She established and edited (with George Clark) **Keramic Studio** from 1899-1929, and executed some very original art porcelain which often featured elaborately carved designs or exquisite crystalline glazes.

American studio potters have developed their craft in a variety of situations. Maria and Julian Martinez lived and worked on the San Ildefonso Pueblo in New Mexico. Their original burnished black pottery reflects ancient traditions. Others like Frank Reuss Kelley, the Overbeck sisters, Gertrud and Otto Natzler, and Henry Varnum Poor created their studio pottery from various backgrounds and each focused attention on a selected aspect of the craft, such as form, glaze, or decoration.

One large group of those men and women identified as studio potters has been closely associated with educational institutions as teachers and artists. Charles Fergus Binns, the first director of the New York College of Clayworking at Alfred, New York; Arthur E. Baggs; Laura Andreson; Charles N. Harder; Maija Grotell; Robert Arneson; and others have all contributed to a more common acceptance of ceramics as a medium of fine art. Often the work of the studio potter reflects **avant-garde** intellectual and conceptual attitudes in art, rather than the mass tastes in decoration to which commercial potteries cater.

48.0 Vase (color plate)
Gertrud and Otto Natzler (working 1939-1972)
Los Angeles, California, 1961
Height 10¼"; Diameter 7⅞"

Wheel-thrown stoneware vase in globular bottle form covered in a dripping blue, green, and gray glaze with crystalline effect. **(E)**

NMAH

48.1 Vase
Mary Louise McLaughlin
(1847-1939)
Cincinnati, Ohio, 1900-1905
Height 4¾"

Wheel-thrown and carved porcelain vase with design of leaf whorls in relief; dark red and pale green spotted glaze; marks on bottom include painted "Losanti", and incised cipher "M^cL", "X", and "326". **(D)**

NMAH

48.2 Vase
Adelaide Alsop Robineau
(1865-1929)
Syracuse, New York, 1908
Height 7⅜"

Carved and incised porcelain vase with relief decoration of crabs and sea plants; streaky matte glazes with crystalline effect. (See also 36: Modern Porcelain) **(E)**

Everson Museum of Art

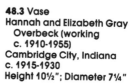

48.3 Vase
Hannah and Elizabeth Gray Overbeck (working c. 1910-1955)
Cambridge City, Indiana
c. 1915-1930
Height 10½"; Diameter 7¼"

Wheel-thrown vase of fine stone-ware with two handles and carved, abstract floral design creating a cameo effect in green and blue matte glazes; impressed "OBK/EH" on bottom. **(D)**

Indianapolis Museum of Art

48.4 Jar
Maria and Julian Martinez (worked together c. 1908-1940)
San Ildefonso Pueblo, New Mexico, c. 1930
Height 9¼"

Coiled and polished earthenware jar decorated with matte black painted serpent and arrowhead design on burnished black background; incised on bottom "Marie [sic]" and "Julian". **(E)**

Private Collection

48.5 Vase
Frank Reuss Kelley
Philadelphia, Pennsylvania, and Norwalk, Connecticut, c. 1925
Height 5½"

Wheel-thrown and modeled bulbous vase of earthenware with narrow mouth and four loop handles at the neck; covered in a deep red drip glaze over a brown ground; incised "Reuss" on bottom. **(B)**

Private Collection

48.6 Plate
Henry Varnum Poor (1888-1971)
Pomona, Rockland County, New York, 1928
Diameter 11"

Round, shallow earthenware plate with plain rim and underglaze-painted duck and water decoration in colors. **(E)**

The Metropolitan Museum of Art

48.7 Figurine
Carl Walters (1883-1955)
Woodstock, New York, 1929
Length 11½"

Modeled earthenware figure of a duck decorated with underglaze reds and yellow on a cream-colored ground; incised signature on bottom. **(E)**

48.8 Vase
Charles M. Harder (1889-1959)
Alfred, New York, 1931
Height 10"

Wheel-thrown stoneware vase with tapering cylindrical form; incised horizontal lines and abstract, modeled surface design. **(D)**

NMAH

48.9 Vase
Maija Grotell (1899-1973)
Bloomfield Hills, Michigan, 1945
Height 17"

Wheel-thrown stoneware vase with tapering cylindrical form; incised horizontal lines and white slip relief in an abstract design. **(E)**

Everson Museum of Art

48.10 Covered Bowl

Peter Voulkos (1924-present)
Archie Bray Foundation, Helena, Montana, 1953
Diameter 13¼"

Wheel-thrown, hemispherical, footed stoneware bowl with cover and high concave cylindrical handle; decorated with white slip whorls against a dark glaze. (E)

NMAH

48.11 Moon Pot
Toshiko Takaezu (born 1922)
Princeton, New Jersey, 1973
Diameter 23"

Hand-formed stoneware sphere with glazes of muted gray and mustard tones. (E)

New Jersey State Museum

48.12 "T Pot"
Robert Arneson (1930-present)
Davis, California, 1969
Height 12"

Modeled earthenware teapot in sculptural "funk art" style, inscribed "Tea, a reception or social gathering in the late afternoon" and covered with colored glazes. **(E)**

Anne Kohs & Associates, Inc.

49 | Tiles

One of the major concerns of those embracing aestheticism in late nineteenth century interior decoration was, "to surround the home and everyday life with objects of true beauty" **(The Decorator and Furnisher, 1882)**. The use of relief-molded, intaglio, and painted tiles was an easy and relatively inexpensive way to introduce the arts of sculpture and printmaking into the home without seeming frivolous. Tiles were, first of all, hygienic because the hard surface was easily cleaned. Secondly, their use introduced color and pattern into the home. Thirdly, the subjects displayed on decorated tiles might "fill the mind with higher thoughts."

From at least the late seventeenth century tiles had been used in some American houses, primarily for fireplace decoration, but also to a limited extent as baseboards and even, in rare instances, as wainscoting in courtly Dutch homes. All tiles used in America prior to the mid-nineteenth century were imported.

Between 1845 and 1855 experiments were carried out in Philadelphia to manufacture Rockingham tiles and in Bennington to produce inlaid tiles. These were not commercially marketed. Inlaid floor tiles and relief-molded fireplace tiles were made for a short time during the 1870s by Messrs. Hyzer and Lewellen of Philadelphia.

The firm of J. and J.G. Low, Chelsea, Massachusetts, may be considered the first to successfully mass-produce art tiles in America. Their initial kiln full of tiles, fired in 1879, in effect marked the beginning of what was to become a very large industry in this country. Prior to 1880 tiles were not generally popular in America. Interest grew steadily, however, until in the years before the First World War production was valued at about $5,000,000 annually, while sales of imported tiles amounted to only $100,000.

John Gardner Low made a number of contributions to the tile industry in America. Of these, his patented invention of the "natural tile," decorated with the impressions of leaves and grasses, is perhaps the most important. The Lows are also well-known for the relief tiles and plaques designed and modeled by Arthur Osborne. Reproductions of the original sculptured designs were made from plaster casts. When the clay was partially dry, the cast was removed and the impression worked by undercutting the design for greater depth.

Of course, these two processes resulted in expensive tiles because of all the handwork involved. Most companies making intaglio tiles used the "dust" process in which powdered clay that had been slightly moistened was subjected to enormous pressure from a die cut with the pattern. These tiles were biscuit-fired, then glazed in a second firing. In one sense, tiles made in this manner are like paintings, except that shading is produced by contour. The variation in color resulted from the depth of the pooled glaze.

In the 1870s, also, the American Encaustic Tiling Company was organized in Zanesville, Ohio (closed 1935), where plain and inlaid encaustic tile (the color is throughout the clay) as well as plain and intaglio glazed tiles with figures, flowers, and popular conventional patterns were made. Campaign tiles of William McKinley and William Jennings Bryan are of political, as well as artistic interest. Many large relief tile panels were designed for A.E.T. Co. by Herman Carl Mueller, who later founded the Mosaic Tile Company with Karl Langenbeck in Zanesville (1894-1967) and, in 1909, organized the Mueller Mosaic Tile Company in Trenton, New Jersey (closed 1938). In Zanesville, Mueller and Langenbeck used perforated patterns to apply colored clay to the surface of the tile. They also produced inlaid and mosaic tiles by a variety of ingenious methods.

By 1900 at least thirty companies had been established for the production of tiles. Of the few that survived beyond the turn of the century, several are significant. The Beaver Falls Art Tile Company, Beaver Falls, Pennsylvania (1886-1930), is noted for its many raised designs of heads and large panels of the Muses. The famous ceramic designers Isaac Broome and William Gallimore worked for the Trent Tile Company of Trenton, New Jersey (1882-1938, now part of Wenczel Tile Company). The antiquarian, Henry Chapman Mercer (1856-1930), began production about 1912 at the Moravian Pottery and Tile Works in Doylestown, Pennsylvania, in an attempt to sustain pottery manufacture as a handcraft. Tiles were made there until 1956. Mercer's methods have recently been revived and the factory reopened as a working museum. Many of the designs for his distinctive relief and intaglio tiles were adapted from medieval and meso-American Indian sources.

Other important tile companies include the United States Encaustic Tile Company, Indianapolis, Indiana (1877-c. 1934); Cambridge Art Tile Works, near Cincinnati (1887-1929); Providential Tile Works, Trenton (1886-1913); and Robertson Art Tile Company, Morrisville, Pennsylvania (established 1890, now Robertson Manufacturing Company).

49.0 Group of Six Tiles (color plate)
J. and J.G. Low Art Tile Works (active 1879-1883; J.G. and J.F. Low
    1883-1902)
Chelsea, Massachusetts, 1881-1885
Sizes vary from 4" x 4" to 8" x 13"

Relief-molded tiles with heads of children, adults, and old people in
various colors. Several are marked with the cipher of Arthur Osborne,
who designed many of the molds for the tiles. **(B-D, small-large)**

NMAH

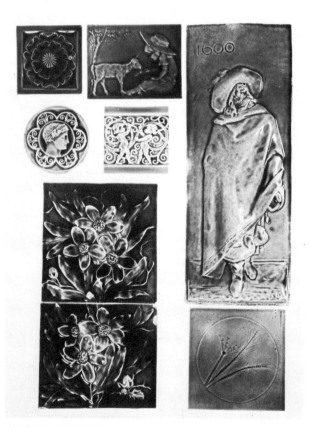

49.1 Group of Eight Tiles
J. and J.G. Low Art Tile Works (active 1879-1883; J.G. and J.F. Low
    1883-1902)
Chelsea, Massachusetts, 1879-1902

Flower tiles 7½" x 7½"

This group of tiles shows the range of work offered by Low. The delicate tile in the lower right was made by the patented "natural process" in which plants were pressed into the damp tile. The long tile bears the initials of Arthur Osborne. **(A-D, small-large)**

NMAH

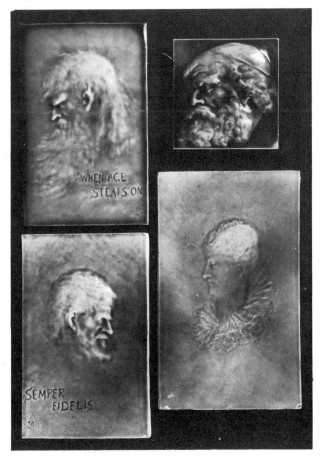

49.2 Group of Four Tiles
J. and J.G. Low Art Tile Works (active 1879-1883; J.G. and J.F. Low 1883-1902)
Chelsea, Massachusetts, c. 1885

Left tiles each 7" x 11"; small tile 6" x 6"; large tile 13" x 8"

Four designs of heads modeled by Arthur Osborne in yellow brown and yellow green. **(D, left two; C, right two)**

NMAH

49.3 Group of Six Tiles
Grueby Faience and Tile Company (active 1895-1910)
Boston, Massachusetts, 1895-1910
4" x 4" and 6" x 6"; small hexagonal tile is 3" on each edge

Matte-glazed tiles in yellow, tan, blue green, green, brown and white; the deer and rosette are relief molded. Grueby's firm is perhaps most famous for its art pottery (See 41: New England Art Pottery), but tiles produced by the company are also very attractive. **(D, landscape; C, flower; B, others)**

NMAH

49.4 Tile
Marblehead Pottery (1905-1936)
Marblehead, Massachusetts
c. 1925
6" x 6"

White earthenware tile hand painted in matte glazes with a decoration of delphiniums in various shades of blue with green and yellow on a cream-colored background and medium blue border. The Marblehead Pottery is best-known for its art vases. (See 41: New England Art Pottery) **(C)**

Private Collection

49.5 Tile
Trent Tile Company (active 1882-1938)
Trenton, New Jersey, 1883-1886
6" x 6"

Relief-molded tile depicting the head of a bearded man in overall golden amber glaze. The design is attributed to Isaac Broome, who had worked previously for Ott and Brewer, and for whom he designed the famous Baseball Vase and bust of Cleopatra. **(B)**

NMAH

49.6 Tile
Providential Tile Works (active 1885-1913)
Trenton, New Jersey, c. 1900
4¼" x 4¼"

High-grade stoneware tile with relief-molded decoration of scrolls arranged in a geometric pattern. Isaac Broome of the Trent Tile Co. and formerly of Ott & Brewer, was the first designer for Providential. **(A)**

Private Collection

49.7 Tile
Mueller Mosaic Tile Company
(active 1909-1938)
Trenton, New Jersey, 1909-1925
4" x 4"

Red earthenware tile with relief
decoration of eight conventional
tulips arranged in a geometric
pattern and glazed with navy
blue and tan. Herman Carl Mueller came to Trenton from Ohio
where he had worked for the
American Encaustic Tiling Co. He
began the Mosaic Tile Company
with Karl Langenbeck in Zanesville. **(A)**

New Jersey State Museum

49.8 Group of Eight Tiles
**Moravian Pottery and Tile Works (c. 1900-1956; recently reactivated
as a working museum)**
Doylestown, Pennsylvania, 1900-1930
Tiles in upper right are 4" x 4"

This group illustrates the variety of tile shapes designed and produced
by Henry Chapman Mercer. Molded in relief of coarse red earthenware, the tiles are glazed in bright reds, yellows, blues, and greens. **(A,
each)**

NMAH

49.9 Group of Five Tiles
American Encaustic Tiling Co. (active 1875-1935)
Zanesville, Ohio, c. 1890-1930
6"x 16"; 4" x 4"; 3" x 3"

These five tiles show a small survey of the types of tiles made by
A.E.T.Co., including terra cotta in relief (the child and ram designed by
Herman Carl Mueller, c. 1890); molded intaglio designs (small McKinley and Hobart tiles from 1896 campaign); and painted faience bird
and tulip tiles made in the 1920s. **(C, top; A, rest)**

NMAH

49.10 Tile
American Encaustic Tile Company (1875-1936)
Zanesville, Ohio, c. 1885
Height 6"; Width 6"

Press-molded square tile with transfer-printed decoration of maiden
and pig and the legend "There was a lady loved all swine" with some
hand coloring; marked "AETCO" on reverse. **(A)**

49.11 Group of Eleven Tiles
Cambridge Tile Manufacturing Co. (1887-1929; from 1887-1889
  known as Cambridge Art Tile Works)
Covington, Kentucky, 1887-1889
6" x 6", 4¼" x 6", or 6" x 9"

Relief-molded tiles with heads and a variety of Classical-Revival patterns of cartouches, scrolls, and swags in various greens, dark brown,
blue gray, and white. Heinrich Binz, a German tilemaker working in
Covington, was one of the three partners in this company. **(A, each)**

NMAH

50 | Modern Tableware

The modern tableware industry includes a number of companies
which were active in the nineteenth century. As in the past, the factories in the twentieth century tended to congregate in two important
areas: Trenton, New Jersey, and East Liverpool, Ohio. In these locations, the raw materials were readily accessible and cheap transportation of finished goods and material was assured.

One of the new entries in the twentieth-century marketplace, Lenox,
Inc., has since become an American institution. Walter Scott Lenox
learned the porcelain business and worked as art director at the Ott &

Brewer Company of Trenton before 1888, and afterwards at Willets Manufacturing Company. He formed the Ceramic Art Company in 1889 at Trenton with Jonathan Coxon, bought out his partner in 1895, and renamed the company Lenox, Inc., in 1906. The first American porcelain tableware ordered by the White House in 1918 for the administration of Woodrow Wilson, former Governor of New Jersey, was made by Lenox. Later, Presidents Franklin Roosevelt and Harry Truman also ordered their table services from Lenox. The company is still in business today producing fine porcelain tableware as well as a line of art wares.

Other prominent Trenton manufacturers working during this century include the Stangl Pottery and the Scammell China Company. J. Martin Stangl worked for the Fulper Pottery of Flemington, New Jersey, as early as 1911, but after a factory fire in 1929, the main business was moved to Trenton. In 1930 Stangl acquired the firm and the emphasis was changed from art pottery to fine earthenware for the table. Production continued until 1972, the year of Stangl's death. Scammell China Company can be traced back to the Trenton China Company, founded in 1859. It was subsequently purchased by Thomas Maddock & Sons Company in 1893 and bought from them in 1923 by six Scammell brothers. A broad line of institutional, restaurant, and home tablewares was manufactured.

Pottery has been made by numerous companies and individuals in East Liverpool, Ohio, since John Koontz first made redware there in 1807. One of the largest of the East Liverpool tableware manufactories is the Homer Laughlin China Company, established in 1869 as Simms and Laughlin. Homer Laughlin bought out his partner by 1877 and the business prospered, employing 137 workers in 1887. After 1897 the name was changed to simply Laughlin China Company. Tableware has always been a major product of the company. In 1905 they built what was then the largest pottery in the world at Newell, Ohio. A very popular line of tableware called "Fiesta Ware" was introduced by the company in 1936. Seventy different forms were made in eleven colors, and two new colors were added when the line was revived in 1968.

A rival in size to Homer Laughlin was the firm of Knowles, Taylor, and Knowles, established in 1870. Their production of tableware and art ware was extremely successful and by 1901 there were thirty-five kilns in operation on ten acres, with more than 700 workers employed. A wide variety of patterns was manufactured in white ware and institutional china. In 1928 Knowles, Taylor, and Knowles was one of eight companies which merged to form the American China Corporation, but the venture failed during the Depression. A large number of other tableware companies in the United States have failed during the twentieth century due to the competition from cheap, imported Japanese porcelain.

50.0 Covered Sugar Bowl (color plate)
Lenox, Inc. (1906-present)
Trenton, New Jersey, 1925-1935
Height 4½"

Covered sugar bowl of molded porcelain in the "Fountain" pattern with a decorative floral band below the shoulder (flower basket and garlands in colored enamels on blue ground) and gilt trim; printed "L" in wreath on bottom. **(A)**

New Jersey State Museum

50.1 Plate
Stangl Pottery Company (1930-1972)
Trenton, New Jersey, 1969
Diameter 10½"

Round plate of molded red earthenware decorated with incised flowers in brown, yellow, green, and orange glazes in "First Love" pattern on a white slip ground; printed marks "Hand Painted" and "Stangl/Trenton, N.J./First Love" on bottom. **(A)**

New Jersey State Museum

50.2 Relish Tray
Buffalo Pottery (1901-1956)
Buffalo, New York, 1908
Length 12"; Width 6½"

Molded, shallow oval tray in olive green semi-vitreous porcelain with transfer-printed decoration of "Ye Olden Times" in black and hand-painted highlights in colored enamels and clear overglaze; printed mark "1908 DELDARE WARE" and buffalo. **(B)**

50.3 Covered Butter Dish
J.S. Taft & Company (1871-1923)
Keene, New Hampshire, 1890-1910
Height 4½"; Diameter 8"

Round underplate of molded white ware with scalloped edge and high domed cover with button knob; all decorated in "Royal Worcester" finish glaze with brown brushed highlights and gilt trim; printed mark on bottom "J.S. Taft, Hampshire Pottery, Keene, N.H." **(A)**

50.4 Cream Pitcher
Homer Laughlin China Company (1877-present)
East Liverpool, Ohio, and Newell, West Virginia, 1936-1971
Width 5⅞"

Footed cream pitcher of molded, buff-colored earthenware with overall dark blue glossy glaze; marked on bottom "Fiesta/Made in USA" and "HL" cipher. **(A)**

Pauline's Antiques

50.5 Serving Dish
Knowles, Taylor, and Knowles (1870-1928)
East Liverpool, Ohio, 1900-1920
Diameter 8"

Round, shallow bowl of semi-vitreous porcelain glazed overall in white and decorated with transfer-printed design of red roses and green leaves, "Ramona" pattern; printed eagle mark in circle, "KTK" cipher above, and "K.T.&K. Co./Ramona." **(A)**

Private Collection

50.6 Cream Pitcher
West End Pottery Company
**   (1893-1934)**
East Liverpool, Ohio, 1900-1915
Height 4½"

Cream pitcher of molded white ironstone glazed in white and decorated with printed pink and blue floral design on black background; printed mark "WEST END POTTERY CO./EAST/LIVERPOOL/ OHIO." **(A)**

Ron's Antiques

Selected Bibliography

Altman, V., and Altman, S. *The Book of Buffalo Pottery.* New York: Crown Publishers, Inc., 1969.

Arnest, B., editor. *Van Briggle Pottery: The Early Years.* Colorado Springs: Colorado Springs Fine Arts Center, 1975.

Barber, E. A. *Pottery and Porcelain of the United States* (third edition, 1901) and *Marks of American Potters* (originally published, 1904), reissued together by Feingold & Lewis (New York), 1977.

———. *Tulipware of the Pennsylvania Germans.* Philadelphia: Patterson & White., 1903. Available in Dover reprint, 1970.

Barnard, J. *Victorian Ceramic Tiles.* London: Studio Vista Publisher, 1972.

Barret, R. C. *Bennington Pottery and Porcelain: A Guide to Identification.* New York: Crown Publishers, Inc., 1958.

Bivins, J., Jr. *The Moravian Potters in North Carolina.* Chapel Hill: The University of North Carolina Press, 1972.

Branin, M. L. *The Early Potters and Potteries of Maine.* Middletown, Conn.: Wesleyan University Press, 1978.

Bray, H. V. *The Potter's Art in California 1885-1955.* Oakland: Oakland Museum of Art, 1978.

Clark, G., and Hughto, M. *A Century of Ceramics in the United States 1878-1978.* New York: E. P. Dutton (in association with the Everson Museum of Art, Syracuse), 1979.

Crawford, J. *Jugtown Pottery: History and Design.* Winston-Salem, N.C.: John F. Blair, Publishers, 1964.

Curtis, P. H. "The Production of Tucker Porcelain 1826-1838: A Reevaluation." *Ceramics in America,* edited by Ian Quimby. Winterthur Conference Report, 1972 (Charlottesville: The University Press of Virginia), pp. 339-374.

Evans, P. *Art Pottery of the United States: An Encyclopedia of Producers and Their Marks.* New York: Charles Scribner's Sons, 1974.

Greer, G. H. *American Stoneware, The Art and Craft of Utilitarian Potters.* Exton, Pa.: Schiffer Publishing Ltd., 1981.

Guilland, H. F. *Early American Folk Pottery.* Philadelphia: Chilton Book Co., 1971 (illustrations from the Index of American Design).

Hood, G. *Bonnin and Morris of Philadelphia: The First American Porcelain Factory 1770-1772.* Chapel Hill: The University of North Carolina Press, 1972.

Hough, W. *An Early West Virginia Pottery.* Washington, D.C.: Smithsonian Institution, 1901. Especially good for the numerous illustrations of potter's tools.

James, A. E. *The Potters and Potteries of Chester County, Pennsylvania.* West Chester, Pa.: Chester County Historical Society, 1945. Reissued by Schiffer Publishing, Exton, Pa., 1978.

Keen, K. *American Art Pottery 1875-1930.* Wilmington: Delaware Art Museum, 1978.

Ketchum, W. C., Jr. *Early Potters and Potteries of New York State.* New York: Funk & Wagnalls, 1970.

Klamkin, M. *American Patriotic and Political China*. New York: Charles Scribner's Sons, 1973.

Kovel, R., and Kovel, T. *The Kovels' Collector's Guide to American Art Pottery*. New York: Crown Publishers, Inc., 1974.

Lehner, L. *Ohio Pottery and Glass: Marks and Manufacturers*. Des Moines, Iowa: Wallace-Homestead Book Co., 1980.

_____. *The Complete Book of American Kitchen and Dinner Wares*. Des Moines, Iowa: Wallace-Homestead Book Co., 1980.

Myers, S. H. *Handcraft to Industry: Philadelphia Ceramics in the First Half of the Nineteenth Century*. Washington, D.C.: Smithsonian Institution Press, 1980.

New Jersey Pottery to 1840. Trenton: New Jersey State Museum, an exhibition March 18-May 12, 1972.

Newlands, D. L. *Early Ontario Potters: Their Craft and Trade*. Toronto: McGraw-Hill Ryerson Ltd., 1979.

Ormond, S., and Irvine, M. E. *Louisiana's Art Nouveau: The Crafts of the Newcomb Style*. Gretna, La.: The Pelican Publishing Co., 1976.

Pear, L. M. *The Pewabic Pottery*. Des Moines, Iowa: Wallace-Homestead Book Co., 1976.

Peck, H. *The Book of Rookwood Pottery*. New York: Crown Publishers, Inc., 1968.

Ramsay, J. *American Potters and Pottery*. New York: Tudor Publishing Co., 1947.

Schwartz, M. D., and Wolfe, R. *A History of American Art Porcelain*. New York: Renaissance Editions, 1967.

Spargo, J. *Early American Pottery and China*. New York: The Century Co., 1926. Reissued by Charles E. Tuttle, Rutland, Vt., 1974.

_____. *The Potters and Potteries of Bennington*. Boston: Houghton Mifflin Co., 1926. Reissued in Dover reprints, 1972.

Stradling, D., and Stradling, J. G., editors. *The Art of the Potter: Redware and Stoneware*. Clinton, N.J.: The Main Street Press, 1977. Compilation of articles which appeared originally in *The Magazine Antiques*.

Viel, L. C. *The Clay Giants: The Stoneware of Red Wing, Goodhue County, Minnesota*. Des Moines, Iowa: Wallace-Homestead Book Co., 1977.

Watkins, L. W. *Early New England Potters and Their Wares*. Cambridge, Mass.: Harvard University Press, 1950. Reprinted by Archon Books, 1968.

Webster, D. B. *Decorated Stoneware Pottery of North America*. Rutland, Vt.: Charles E. Tuttle, 1971.

_____. *Early Canadian Pottery*. Greenwich, Conn.: New York Graphic Society, 1971.

Wiltshire, W. E., III. *Folk Pottery of the Shenandoah Valley*. New York: E.P. Dutton, 1975.

Zug, C. G., III. *The Traditional Pottery of North Carolina*. Chapel Hill: The University of North Carolina, Ackland Museum, 1981.

Acknowledgments

The authors wish to express their appreciation to the following persons for their kind assistance with this book: Susan Myers and Regina Blaszczyk, National Museum of American History, Smithsonian Institution; Suzanne Corlette, New Jersey State Museum; Nancy and Gary Stass; Kathleen S. and George R. Hamell; Jim Biden and John Van Doren; Catherine Lippert, Indianapolis Museum of Art; Lyndon C. Viel; Donald Blake Webster, Royal Ontario Museum; Neville Thompson and the staff of the Library, Henry Francis du Pont Winterthur Museum.

Although abbreviated source credits appear in the individual entries of the book, the following complete credits should be noted: (30.0) The National Museum of American History, Gift of the Barra Foundation; (31.2) The Brooklyn Museum, Dick S. Ramsay Fund; (31.3, 32.4) The Philadelphia Museum of Art, Gift of Mrs. Robert John Hughes; (33.5) The Metropolitan Museum of Art, Rogers Fund, 1914; (34.3) The Brooklyn Museum, Gift of Frederick Chace; (34.5) The Metropolitan Museum of Art, Gift of Mr. and Mrs. Franklin M. Chace, 1969; (37.6) The Metropolitan Museum of Art, Gift of Wells M. Sawyer, 1945; (46.5) The Brooklyn Museum, Gift of Arthur W. Clement; (48.6) The Metropolitan Museum of Art (Purchase, 1928), Gift of Edward C. Moore Jr.

Photo Credits

1. Decorative Arts Photographic Collection
(16.13)

2. Indianapolis Museum of Art
(13.8, 13.12, 17.9)

3. New Jersey State Museum, Joseph Crilley, photographer.
(5.0, 9.6, 21.3, 24.0, 24.4, 25.2, 25.3, 26.0, 26.1, 26.2, 27.0, 27.1, 28.2, 28.3, 28.4, 28.5, 29.1, 29.2, 33.4, 35.0, 35.1, 35.3, 35.5, 35.6, 35.7, 35.8, 36.4, 36.5, 36.6, 36.7, 36.8, 37.11, 48.11, 49.7, 50.0, 50.1)

4. Rochester Museum and Science Center, William G. Frank, photographer.
(1.2, 7.0, 7.1, 7.3, 7.4, 14.1, 19.6)

5. Sam Sweezy, photographer.
(21.0)

Index